COROT

BY

ETHEL BIRNSTINGL
AND
ALICE POLLARD

WITH TWENTY-SEVEN ILLUSTRATIONS

METHUEN & CO.
36 ESSEX STREET W.C.
LONDON

First published in 1904

CONTENTS

CHAPTER I

BIRTH AND PARENTAGE

Birth—Parents' occupation—Early childhood—School at Rouen—
M. Jeunegon—Fails to make his mark—Leaves school—Returns
to Paris—Apprenticed to a draper—Becomes town traveller—
Change of career—First studies in art—Michallon—The Studio
Suisse—First sketch—Gratitude to Michallon—Victor Bertin as

CHAPTER II

STUDENT LIFE

First visit to Rome—Friends and companions—Life in Rome—
Friendship with Aligny — First Salon pictures — Return to
France—The house at Ville d'Avray—Methods of work—The
Salon of 1831—Change of style—Short tour in France—Chartres
—Italian influence—The Salon of 1833—The "Catacombs"—
Corot's excessive modesty—His first medal—Second visit to
Italy—Recalled to France—"Hagar in the Wilderness"—
"St. Jérôme" — The "Baptism of Christ" in the Church of

CHAPTER III

SUCCESS—MIDDLE AGE—OLD AGE AND DEATH

The Quai Voltaire— Français—The first purchaser— Death of
Corot senior—Third visit to Italy—Love of Nature—The Legion
of Honour—First Hanging Committee of the Salon—Universal
Exhibition of 1855—Corot visits London—The salons—Death
of M. Dutilleux—Siege of Paris—Corot's large contributions to
public charities — Sketching tour in North of France —The
médaille d'honneur— Gérôme — Special gold medal for the
"Master"—English co-operation—Geoffroy Dechaume—Death
of Mme. Sennegon—Corot's ill-health—Presentation of the

CONTENTS

CHAPTER IV

FUNERAL—EXHIBITION—MEMORIALS

CHAPTER V

COROT THE MAN

CHAPTER VI

COROT THE ARTIST

CHAPTER VII

CRITICISM, CONTEMPORARY AND LATER

CONTENTS

CHAPTER VIII

METHODS OF PAINTING

CHAPTER IX

FRESCOES AND DECORATIVE WORK

LIST OF ILLUSTRATIONS

The pictures against which no source is mentioned are from
the British Museum.

COROT

CHAPTER I

BIRTH AND PARENTAGE

Birth—Parents' occupation—Early childhood—School at
Rouen—M. Jeunegon—Fails to make his mark—Leaves
school—Returns to Paris—Apprenticed to a draper—
Becomes town traveller—Change of career—First studies
in art—Michallon—The Studio Suisse—First sketch—
Gratitude to Michallon—Victor Bertin as master.

JEAN BAPTISTE CAMILLE COROT was
born in Paris on July 20th, 1796. His father
occupied some small post under Government,
the exact nature of which is uncertain. His
mother was a milliner, and managed a business
in the Rue du Bac, where she acquired a semi-
fashionable reputation. Jean Baptiste was an
only son, but his mother bore her husband also
two daughters. Of the characters of these
girls little is known. The elder married a
M. Sennegon, lived to a good old age, and
died but a few weeks before her famous brother.

B

After the death of their father, the brother and sister were in the habit of passing some part of each year together in their villa at Ville d'Avray. M. Corot had bought this villa when his children were young, and left it to them as a joint possession at his death.

Madame Froment, the younger daughter, died soon after her marriage and left no children. Her dowry, therefore, reverted to her family—a fact of the greatest importance to Camille, as it was this sum which formed the basis of the allowance made him by his father, in order, as we shall afterwards relate more fully, to enable him to give up the trade to which he had been put, and which he hated, and to devote himself to the art he so greatly loved.

If Camille showed any unusual qualities as a child, these do not seem to have made sufficient impression on his commonplace parents to have been recorded by them, for we can discover none of the anecdotes usually to be found regarding the childhood of every famous man or woman. That he was a very amiable child is more than probable, since in adult life the gentleness and sweetness of his disposition struck everyone with whom he came into contact. We hear of rejoicings at the birth of the boy, and would gladly believe that other than merely material hopes prompted that rejoicing; but from the views of life expressed by M. and Madame Corot when the child had grown to be a man, we are more inclined to think that visions of a capable son with commercial instincts, ready in the future to carry yet further the prosperous business the parents had built up lay at the root of the pleasure shown at his arrival.

We smile when we realise how these hopes were defeated, and we wonder at the blindness of the parents, who never really recognised nor valued their child's genius, and would so infinitely have preferred a son of the normal and commonplace kind, such as doubtless their neighbours on all sides rejoiced over.

It was probably owing to M. Corot's honourable employment under Government that he owed the privilege of being able to send his son to a school at Rouen at half the usual fees. This privilege he embraced eagerly, and from the age of eleven (1807) until that of sixteen (1812) Camille remained a pupil in the Rouen Lycée. One of the conditions of these "scholarships" was that the parents of a pupil should find someone residing in the neighbourhood of the school who would act as their repre-

sentative and make himself responsible for the
scholar. A friend of the Corots, M. Jeunegon,
undertook this duty towards young Corot, and
appears to have considered himself responsible,
amongst other things, for the way in which the
boy occupied his holidays and his out-of-school
hours. He was in the habit therefore of taking
Camille for long walks, during which, however, being himself of a taciturn disposition, he
made little attempt to entertain his young companion, contenting himself with taking him by
solitary by-paths, under branching trees or
along the water's edge. These sombre wan-
derings, when twilight filled the woods with
mystery, gave free rein to the just awakening
imagination of the lad. We can guess, from
the results in his later years, with what forms
he peopled the silent glades around him and
judge of the rich soil of the boy's mind into
which the seeds of romance fell and flourished.

Dumesnil attributes to these early influences
the dreamy tendencies of the artist's future,
although Corot himself is inclined to attribute
them to the first years which he spent at his
parents' home at the Ville d'Avray. Here, he
tells us, that as a young man, night after night
found him dreamily watching the mists as they
rose and spread over the pond until they

Corot

LITTLE BOOKS ON ART

Demy 16*mo.* 2*s.* 6*d. net.*

SUBJECTS

MINIATURES. ALICE CORKRAN
BOOKPLATES. EDWARD ALMACK
GREEK ART. H. B. WALTERS
ROMAN ART. H. B. WALTERS
THE ARTS OF JAPAN. MRS. C. M. SALWEY
JEWELLERY. C. DAVENPORT
CHRIST IN ART. MRS. H. JENNER
OUR LADY IN ART. MRS. H. JENNER
CHRISTIAN SYMBOLISM. H. JENNER
ILLUMINATED MSS. J. W. BRADLEY
ENAMELS. MRS. NELSON DAWSON
FURNITURE. EGAN MEW

ARTISTS

ROMNEY. GEORGE PASTON
DÜRER. L. JESSIE ALLEN
REYNOLDS. J. SIME
WATTS. MISS R. E. D. SKETCHLEY
HOPPNER. H. P. K. SKIPTON
TURNER. FRANCES TYRRELL-GILL
HOGARTH. EGAN MEW
BURNE-JONES. FORTUNÉE DE LISLE
LEIGHTON. ALICE CORKRAN
REMBRANDT. MRS. E. A. SHARP
VELASQUEZ. WILFRID WILBERFORCE and A. R. GILBERT
VANDYCK. MISS M. G. SMALLWOOD
DAVID COX. ARTHUR TOMSON
HOLBEIN. BEATRICE FORTESCUE
COROT. ETHEL BIRNSTINGL and MRS. A. POLLARD
MILLET. NETTA PEACOCK
CLAUDE. E. DILLON
GREUZE AND BOUCHER. ELIZA F. POLLARD
RAPHAEL. A. R. DRYHURST

LITTLE BOOKS ON ART
GENERAL EDITOR: CYRIL DAVENPORT

COROT

gradually enveloped the whole landscape. The vagueness of their intangible forms, rising and falling, opening and closing in again under the mystic beams of a pale moonlight, exercised a fascination over Corot that lasted his whole life through—a fascination of which we can find traces in most of his work.

This same pond, which doubtless formed the inspiration of the pools which adorn nearly all Corot's canvases, was just outside the Corot property at the side of the garden. A pond, probably the same, still exists there, and year by year it is the scene of an artists' fête, held not actually to commemorate Corot, but at which he is doubtless still remembered.

Camille's schooldays appear to have passed with as great a lack of incident as did those of his yet earlier years. His name did not once appear on the prize-list of his school during all the six or seven years of his stay there; he did not even attain a single mark of distinction in drawing. What matter for wonderment is here! So strong a leaning towards art, so passionate a love of nature—a love which sought and found so adequate a mode of expression in later years, but which at the moment when it began to stir within him was dumb! Did the boy perhaps, even then, as afterwards during his apprenticeship to trade, make pictures upon the reverse side of his exercises? Was this really the cause of his failure to make any mark upon his school during the whole course of his stay? In truth, such drawing as the boy was taught may never have appeared to him to bear even the most distant relationship to the pictures of his dreams. Doubtless he failed to see his own figure as the central one of his dreams, or to realise the possibility of his powers to create and perpetuate for all time the glories even then forming in his young mind.

At the age of sixteen Camille left Rouen and returned to Paris, where his father at once apprenticed him to a draper to learn the trade and to acquire those business habits which were to fit him for his future responsible position as "head of a mercantile house." Even Corot's warmest admirers cannot claim for him that he shone in the character of draper's assistant. Perhaps his gentle temperament gave him patience to endure for eight years an occupation that he detested. But it did not prevent him from dreaming over the counters and serving customers in so perfunctory a manner that they raised complaints against him to his employer. This gentleman at

LE BOUQUET D'ARBRES

length, hopeless of making anything of him indoors, transferred him to the post of town traveller, and this change of position led to the climax.

At that period in France olive-green was the fashionable colour in materials, and was greatly sought after. One day the young traveller returned with great elation to his master; he had at length sold a piece of cloth! It was olive-green! M. Delalain was in despair. "Do I keep travellers that they may sell olive-green cloth to outsiders when our own customers are tearing each other to pieces to procure some of it? The duty of a traveller is to palm off last season's goods as the latest novelty." This opened Corot's eyes to the actual situation. He was expected to lie! He went forthwith to his father and placed the matter before him, confessing at last the desire of his heart, and begging his parent's permission to become a painter.

In affixing M. Delalain's name to the above story we must confess that we may be doing an injustice to the memory of a worthy gentleman. The fact is that Corot had two employers, and it is impossible to say with which of the two the green cloth episode is connected. Dumesnil tells us that Camille entered on his

business career under M. Delalain, in the Rue
St. Honoré, and ended it with M. Ratier, in the
Rue de Richelieu ; and of the second employer
he writes that he was a man full of indulgence
for the youth's desire to paint—a desire which
he had never concealed, but had on the contrary
followed on every occasion, hiding his drawings
when necessary under the counter. This account would make M. Ratier the hero of the
green cloth—a supposition which does not
accord with the other characteristics related
of him. But Corot's biographers differ as to
details, and we are unable to obtain evidence
enough to enable us to decide between them.
If it be true that the second employer was a
man of sympathy, who not only tolerated
Camille's habit of sketching in season and out
of season, but also countenanced his young
assistant's attendance—unknown to his people
—at an evening art school (the Studio Suisse),
where he studied from the life, it is not difficult to believe that it was consideration for
his employé which led to his transference to
the post of town traveller. We may even go
further and see in the master's expressed despair at ever making the boy into a successful
merchant an indirect method of helping him to

carry out his own desire of leaving trade and devoting himself to art.

We have no actual proof that Camille ever attended a night school; and, indeed, the conditions of dependence in which his parents held him make it seem very improbable that he would have been able to do so without their knowledge. At the same time, it was undoubtedly during the period of his apprenticeship that Corot made the acquaintance of the young painter Michallon, who afterwards gained renown by carrying off the first Prix de Rome awarded for historical landscape. It does not appear probable that the young men met either in the draper's shop or in the house of Camille's parents, and this meeting with Michallon certainly gives colour to the account of Corot's visits to the Studio Suisse —a studio of great reputation at the time, and therefore exceedingly likely to have been a favourite haunt of Michallon. Albert Wolff tells us that there were many storms before the father's consent was obtained to his son's following the profession of an artist. Camille had served the draper eight years before the dénouement recorded above took place, and this long period of inefficiency must have proved even to his reluctant father the improbability of his making any success in trade. But he would not give up his hope without a struggle. Victor Bertin, the artist, was called in to give an opinion as to any artistic talent latent in the young Corot, and on his pronouncing his decided conviction that the talent was there, Corot *aîné* gave an ungracious and unwilling consent to his son's exchanging a "useful and honourable career" for that which, in his eyes, was but a useless pastime.

"I have given your sisters dowries," he said, "but for you I had destined a far larger portion, one which would have set you up in a respectable business for life. But for the career which you have chosen I can give you no capital. I will make you an allowance of £60 a year, and with that you must be content. Since it must be so, take it and be happy." Camille was delighted. He flung his arms around his father and thanked him with deep emotion. "You make me more than happy!" he exclaimed.

In relating this anecdote Wolff comments on the fact that it was Bertin who discovered the talent in young Corot, and remarks that "it was the best thing Bertin ever did for posterity." Bertin's idea of "making something of the lad" was to try and turn him into a second edition of himself, but this young pupil was one of Nature's geniuses, and in spite of much bad teaching, he rose above his fellows, and penetrating the cloud with which tradition had obscured her, worked his way to Truth.

After reading this authenticated account of the struggle between father and son, is it possible to believe that the elder Corot was himself a man with some artistic instincts? And yet one of his biographers tells us that this very man interested himself greatly in the theatre, and indeed even wrote a play which had a fairly long and successful run at the Français. We have ourselves examined the list of plays produced at the Français from its foundation, but without finding the name of Corot amongst the authors; but Mme. van Rensselaer, who is responsible for the assertion, corroborates it by the following story. One of the actors, she says, called at the house in the Rue du Bac, but was informed that the master was engaged. "I called on M. Corot," he said later to a colleague, "but I was unable to see him; he was occupied in 'composing' a head-dress of mousseline de soie."

But to return to the story of the artist. Camille wasted no time after obtaining his father's consent to a change of profession, but hastening at once to a shop he purchased the necessary materials, and without even waiting to choose an inspiring point of view, settled himself down on the quay, nearly opposite his father's house, and began to paint his first picture.

This picture—the Seine, with a view of the city in the distance—was always to be found in after years hanging in the artist's studio, and was an object of real affection to him up to the day of his death. Many of his canvases served him for more than one picture, the earlier effort being effaced and replaced with another subject, but this one was almost sacred in his eyes, and remained entirely untouched. He used to show it with pride and pleasure to every visitor and recount with emotion the history of its execution. Naturally enough, when the young man was settled at his new work, his mother's employées came in great curiosity to see how "Master Camille" was getting on. One of these girls, "Mlle. Rose" he called her, remained a friend and visitor all her life, and Corot used to sigh in his later days over the ravages which time had wrought both in him and in the companion of his youth, although it had spared his painting. "See," he would exclaim, "this is as fresh as the day and hour

DANS LES DUNES

on which I painted it, but where is our youth, Mlle. Rose's and mine?"

But pictures painted by the light of nature alone were not considered possible in those days, so Corot proceeded to choose a master. What more natural than that he should place himself under Michallon, who was already his friend? In writing to one of his biographers Corot said that he "left school at eighteen (in 1812) and was in business for eight years"; so if, as is probable, he went to Michallon's studio at once, it would have been in the year 1820.

Michallon's work, old-fashioned and stereotyped as it appears to us, was nevertheless far less conventional than that of Valenciennes, and in truth, by careful study we find in him signs of the forthcoming new school. In later life Corot himself acknowledges a debt of gratitude to his first master for the precepts which he had instilled. "To stand face to face with Nature; to render her with exactitude; to paint what you see and reproduce the impression you have yourself received," these were his orders.

"I made my first drawing from nature at Arcueil," says Corot, "under the eye of the painter whose only advice to me was to render with the utmost fidelity everything that I saw before me. His lesson has been useful; it has

remained the invariable background of my disposition—a disposition always inclined to
accuracy."

Michallon died in September, 1822, and
Corot's next master was Victor Bertin, who
undoubtedly exercised a lasting influence on his
pupil's work. Bertin himself was a painter of
historical or classical landscape, and worked
in the most approved academic manner. He
taught Corot to draw with accuracy—the result
of which teaching is clearly to be found in some
of his architectural drawings—and put him
through such a severe course of classical composition that even Corot's latest work shows
traces of it. In every landscape the figures,
without which he used to say a landscape was
uninhabitable, are placed with a regard to
symmetry which is decidedly more "classical"
than natural. Courbet evidently regarded Corot
as a classical painter spoilt, for he describes
him as "the man who always painted the same
nymphs eternally dancing in the same landscape."

Corot remained as Bertin's pupil for two
years, but does not appear to have set much
store himself by the teaching which he received.

CHAPTER II

STUDENT LIFE

First visit to Rome—Friends and companions—Life in
Rome—Friendship with Aligny—First Salon pictures—
Return to France—The house at Ville d'Avray—
Methods of work—The Salon of 1831—Change of Style
—Short tour in France—Chartres—Italian influence—
The Salon of 1833—The "Catacombs"—Corot's exces-
sive modesty—His first medal—Second visit to Italy—
Recalled to France—"Hagar in the wilderness"—"St.
Jérôme"—The "Baptism of Christ" in the Church of
St. Nicholas du Chardonnet.

IN 1825 he went with Bertin to Rome, and
from thence wrote to a friend that he had
not learnt to draw at all. His idea of drawing
differed essentially from that of his master.
Bertin gave strict attention to detail and to
accuracy of line ; Corot aimed at obtaining the
whole effect in a quick sketch. From 1825 to
1828 the young painter remained in Rome in
company with Aligny, Edouard Bertin (brother
of Victor Bertin), and Robert, who together
with some others formed a kind of French
Academy, with Pierre Guérin as director.

According to Dumesnil, the special characteristic of the work of this Italian period of Corot's was its accuracy; nothing was left to the imagination! Can one imagine Corot ever falling into this defect? Rather are we inclined to believe him ready at any moment of his life to offer a sacrifice at the Altar of the Unknown God — the God whom, had he been desired to name, he would have called Imagination.

That Corot at the time of his first visit to Italy was perfectly aware of his own defects and limitations is evident from a letter he wrote to M. Silvestre, which relates to his first attempt at independent work in Rome. "I had spent two winters," he writes, "with M. Bertin, learning so little that on my arrival in Rome I could not draw at all. Two men stopped to chat together. I began to sketch them, part at a time—the head, for instance. They separated, and I had nothing but some bits of head on my paper. Some children were sitting on the steps of a church. I began again. Their mother called them away, and my book would be full of ends of noses, foreheads, and tresses of hair. I determined that I would not come home again another time without a complete piece of work; and I tried for the first time a drawing *par*

masse, a rapid drawing, the only kind possible.
I set myself, then, to outline, in the twinkling
of an eye, the first group I found ; if it only
stayed a short time, I had at any rate caught
the character, the general *désinvolture ;* if it
stayed long enough I could get the details.   I
made a number of these exercises, and I have
even succeeded in catching, in a few lines on a
scrap of paper at the bottom of my hat, the
ballets and scenic decorations of the opera."

The little body of young painters, the
" French Academy," formed a gay little party
in Rome.   They were in the habit of frequenting
two restaurants, sometimes assembling at the
Café Grec and sometimes at the Restaurant
della Lepre.

At these meetings Corot was always welcome,
being a thoroughly " good fellow," and having,
moreover, a melodious voice much in demand
for the singing of

> "Je sais attacher les rubans,
>   Je sais comment poussent les roses,"

and other favourite sentimental ballads of the
day.

But although ready to accept him as a play-
mate, Corot's companions refused to take him
seriously as an artist until one day when Aligny

c

found him working at his study of the Coliseum,
and pronounced it to be better than anything
which had been done since Claude Lorrain.
This work was exhibited twenty years after in
the Salon of 1849, and then achieved a great
success.

Meanwhile Aligny sought a closer intercourse
with the young painter. "Perhaps, M. Corot,"
he said, "we might sometimes work together.
I may be able to teach you something, and I
shall most certainly gain by your companionship." Corot, always modest, always filled
with gratitude for any encouragement, never
forgot Aligny's offer of friendship, and treated
him with never-failing veneration and respect.
Nearly fifty years after these Roman days, in
the early twilight of a cold, snowy morning,
there was a funeral at Mont Parnasse. But
a few persons were present, and amongst these,
shivering with the cold, was Corot, paying
what he described as a *devoir*—a sacred debt.

In 1827 Corot sent from Rome two pictures
to the Salon. The first of these, "The
Roman Campagna," was afterwards used, in a
way not unusual with the artist, as a canvas for
another picture, but number two, "Vue prise
à Narni," remained in his own possession until
his death, when it was sold to M. Lemaître

for 2,300 francs. Both pictures were hung, and Corot, writing from Rome in March, 1828, says: "One of my friends has just received the *Petit Journal* of the Salon—'M. Corot: 221, 222, colouring good, piquant effect, transparency; we recommend him to draw better and to vary the forms of his trees.' After all I haven't much to complain of so far as the Salon is concerned."

In the same letter he speaks of his probable return to Paris in September, and says that he contemplates travelling a little in Italy before leaving for home.

Between 1828 and 1831 there were no exhibitions at the Salon, and Corot seems to have spent the years partly in travel, visiting chiefly the coast towns on the north of France, and partly at work in his Paris studio.

The "studio" changed its locality more than once, the painter having lived successively at 39, Rue Neuve des Petitschamps; at 15, Quai Voltaire; 10, Rue des Beaux-Arts; and 58, Rue de la Faubourg-Poissonnière. In this latter place he is said to have had a modest living-apartment on the first floor and a studio on the fourth. "It is natural," he said, "to ascend for work and logical to descend for rest. In work the mind is exalted, in sleep the body seeks a lowly attitude."

In addition to his Paris rooms Corot also had his share of the little family villa at Ville d'Avray. This little country house became famous as the focus around which so much of his work centred.

Near the house was a pond, which, if it did not actually itself figure in the many pictures to which it has been assigned, certainly served the artist for more than one inspiration. Close by, too, was an inn, and this was undoubtedly often reproduced in the many sketches made by Corot of Ville d'Avray. In later years he used to frequent this little inn daily at the hour of déjeuner, and there, too, was always to be found a meal and a hearty welcome for any guest who came to visit him in his bachelor home.

After the death of M. and Mme. Corot the villa at Ville d'Avray was shared by Camille and the Sennegons, his sister and her husband, and dearly as he loved his sister, the presence of her husband always exercised a kind of restraint upon Corot and made him feel an interloper in his own house.

At the Ville d'Avray Corot never had a studio ; the idea of building him one never

THE GOATHERD

seems to have occurred to his parents, so that all his painting there was done either in his own bedroom or out of doors. When seized with a desire to paint a picture which necessitated a studio, he would set off for his Paris rooms in hot haste so as not to lose an impression.

This is how he describes the process of transferring impressions gained outside to the canvas ready for them in his studio. "When I come back from an excursion, I invite Nature to come and pass a few days in my house. Then my madness sets in. With my brush in my hand I go out nutting through the woods, in my studio ; and there also I can hear the birds singing and the trees rustling in the wind ; and I can see the streams and the rivers flowing on, carrying thousands of mirror pictures of sky and earth ; and the sun rises and sets for me in my own house ! "

In 1831 Corot sent four works to the Salon, and all were accepted. Of these three belong both by subject and by treatment to the Italian period of his work, but the fourth, " Vue prise dans la forêt de Fontainebleau," marks the beginning of an entire change of style and of method of work.

When we remember that Corot began life as

an artist at an unusually late age, that he was
always slow in developing, that his temperament led him to accept guidance and direction
in all the affairs of his private life to an extent
which came perilously near to injuring him
in his professional work, we ask ourselves
if this same temperament, these same conditions may not be held accountable for the
want of individuality and distinction shown in
his early work, and for his disinclination to
make a determined attack on the old classical
methods in which he had been trained. We
are inclined to think that it is so, and even to
go further and suggest that the painter's easy
circumstances, the very fact that once started
on his career he had never one moment of
struggle, that his small allowance from his
father sufficed and more than sufficed for his
wants — that all these conditions made him
easy-going to the point of indifference. This
attitude of mind is apparent in all his work.
Corot paints Nature in her calm, everyday
moods ; all is serene, all is normal, all would
be, but for the magic of the artist, commonplace. An art critic looking at a collection
of French paintings once said, " Corot never
painted Nature in a convulsion. Look at that
landscape ; it is calm, still, sunny." Corot's

landscapes are always so. When he was painting, had a thunderstorm come up, he would have said, "Bien, now we will put up our paints and wait till the storm is over." And when the landscape had resumed its usual appearance, Corot would have gone on with his work.

This was his attitude towards life, as well as towards art. During his absence from Paris in 1830 on his tour to the north of France, the little revolution broke out which dethroned Charles X. and placed Louis Philippe in his place, so that on Corot's return he found the barricades up and bullets whistling everywhere. Finding it impossible to paint a picture of the "Pont au Change" with the streets full of combatants, he packed up his palette and easel and hurried to Chartres, where he occupied himself with painting the Cathedral, and waited until Paris was quiet again.

But whether or no we are right in our surmises as to the causes which kept Corot under the classical influences so long, there can be no doubt that the break had been made at last, and from henceforth Corot develops slowly but surely his own style, which was to end in a realism as opposed to his early classical method as his own later ideas of "accuracy" were opposed to those of his masters, Michallon and Bertin. After each successive visit to Italy, and of these there were several, Corot relapses to some extent into his classical manner, and for many years his landscapes are peopled with "nymphs" instead of peasants, adorned with "temples" instead of cottages. But in this first "study" in the Forest of Fontainebleau (there were many afterwards) we note the beginning of the new man. Corot has found himself.

In 1833 (the next Salon) he exhibited again, and, indeed, from this time forward there was never (with one exception) an exhibition held at the Salon where he was not represented. Indeed, Corot was one of the few great artists of his day who, in spite of its injustices and many shortcomings, treated the Salon from first to last with consideration and respect. Until the year of his death he always submitted work, and that of his best, and when the busy hand lay at rest, it was found that even in the failing health of the last few months of his life Corot had not forgotten the Salon, and two pictures were ready for the forthcoming exhibition.

Yet for many years the annual struggle, which he always dreaded, brought him nothing

but disappointment. M. Desbarrolles writes in
1844: " He is never seen—he is always put out
of sight, in the dark galleries called the Catacombs. We will prove this. Where was his
' Hagar ' put? In the Catacombs. His ' View
of the Tyrol '? Catacombs. His ' Little Apple
Gatherers '? Catacombs. His ' Nymphs at the
Bath'? Catacombs. His ' Flute Player'? Catacombs."

What, then, gave him courage to face year
by year an ordeal from which many of his
contemporaries shrank? Was it not his ex-
ceeding modesty? Not that he underrated his
own artistic capacity, but that the entire
absence of self-consciousness and personal
vanity led him to attribute his failures to the
personality shown in his work ; in other words,
to the method he took to express his meaning.
When at length the long-deserved, yet long-
withheld, success was attained and Corot's
pictures found favour with the general public,
his satisfaction expressed itself in the following words : "It is the public taste that has
changed, not my work; my methods, my execution, that is all as it was from the beginning; I have persevered, and at last I have
conquered."

His picture, "Madeleine en prière," exhibited

at the Salon of 1833, won him a medal of the second class, and 1834 saw three more of his canvases at the exhibition.

Soon afterwards he joined a friend, M. Grandjean, in another visit to Italy, keeping this time to the north and visiting Venice, but not Rome. He was in Venice when he received a letter from his father complaining of his long absence from home and asking him to return. In great doubt as to what to do, Corot showed the letter to Leopold Robert, a friend of the old days in Rome, and asked his advice. "Go," said Robert, "your parents are old, do not disappoint them." Corot did not hesitate, but sending word to Bertin not to expect him at Rome, he returned to France, taking with him, however, four pictures, all of which show the recrudescence of the classical influence. Amongst them was "Hagar in the Wilderness," the first of his religious pictures. Of these there were several, but they attracted little attention, although some few critics ranked them amongst those of the first importance. A "St. Jérôme" was presented by the painter to the church at Ville d'Avray, and (in 1843) he painted for the baptistery chapel of the Church of St. Nicholas du Chardonnet a large composition of the "Baptism of Christ."

Of this work M. Silvestre remarks: "There can be no doubt of his having painted this picture after his second or third journey to Italy. The landscape (on the left as you enter the chapel) in which the baptism of Christ is represented, entirely recalls in style and character the first drawings that he did when he was with Aligny in the *agro romano* under the clear Italian sky. The whole is a large panel, well filled with trees of a delicate foliage, a river, and, in the far distance, the buildings of a proud city. But the most extraordinary feature of this work is the *figures*, of which there are nine, besides the angel hovering in the sky; they are all life-size, well grouped, and in fine attitudes, and executed in such a manner that a true historical painter need not have hesitated to sign them. This painting is a revelation of his power and aptitude for the 'Grand Art' as Titian, Poussin, and the real great masters, including Rembrandt, understood it."

CHAPTER III

SUCCESS—MIDDLE AGE—OLD AGE AND DEATH

The Quai Voltaire—Français—The first purchaser—Death of Corot senior—Third visit to Italy—Love of nature—The Legion of Honour—First Hanging Committee of the Salon—Universal Exhibition of 1855—Corot visits London—The salons—Death of M. Dutilleux—Siege of Paris—Corot's large contributions to public charities—Sketching tour in north of France — The "médaille d'honneur" — Gérôme — Special gold medal for the "Master"—English co-operation—Geoffroy Dechaume—Death of Mme. Sennegon—Corot's ill-health—Presentation of the medal—Last exhibits for the Salon—Increased ill-health—Death.

ON his return to Paris from the second Italian visit, Corot established himself at 15, Quai Voltaire, and this remained his town headquarters for the next fourteen years. During the first ten years of this period he continued to exhibit steadily at the Salon, but he found little appreciation from the general public, and still less from his own family.

It must have been about 1840 that he received

DAPHNIS ET CHLOÉ

the first recognition of his genius from his father, for the following story is told with regard to the "Petit Berger," now in the art gallery at Metz.

One of his pupils, Français, who had been with him for some years, made a lithograph of the picture, and Corot showed the copy to his father, who had seen the original many times without remarking any special charm in it. "Tiens," he said, on seeing the lithograph, "that's nice! I will invite M. Français to dinner." When Français arrived, many eulogies and congratulations were showered on him. "But now," said Corot the elder, "our Camille—has he really anything in him?" "He is a great master," replied the pupil, smiling; and as a result of the interview Camille's father suggested to his wife the propriety of raising their son's allowance a little!

It was not until 1847 that Corot found his first purchaser. This was a M. Dutilleux, of Arras, an ardent admirer of Corot, and a collector. Having seen one of his paintings in the Salon, and desiring to possess it, he welcomed the opportunity of making a closer acquaintance with the artist, and sent him a warm invitation to visit him at Arras. The following reply is but another proof of the artist's great simplicity of character and lack of personal vanity.

" PARIS,

"*le* 14 *jan.*, 1849.

" SIR,

"Your letter has given me great pleasure. I thank you very much for the renewal of your invitation to go and see you. Be certain, sir, that if it be only for a few days, I shall give myself the pleasure of making this little journey as soon as the fine weather returns. I have communicated the contents of your letter to my mother, who, after the expressions it contains, can no longer refuse me the permission to fly to you. We shall then be able to admire together that beautiful Nature who presents herself in so ravishing a form to all who seek her. Awaiting the pleasure of seeing you either at Arras or in Paris, "I am, etc.,

"C. COROT."

But we believe that, after all, this visit was not paid until a much later date, when the artist became his own master. Corot was always a dutiful son, and his parents, although failing to understand or appreciate his genius, seem to have been very reluctant to have him out of their sight, and shortly after this invitation had been given and accepted, Corot's father died, and thereafter the son only left his mother when obliged to go further afield than the little Ville d'Avray to seek studies for his pictures.

In 1843, before his father's death, the artist had made a third visit to Italy, remaining there about six months. Italy always renewed in him the classical associations and ideas in which he had been trained; but in Italy also, and especially during this third visit, he "brought to perfection his study of the 'values of tones,'" so that, as Silvestre expresses it, "he could arrange judiciously the scheme of a landscape, precisely as if he were putting together the fragments of a mosaic." In his treatment, too, of *light* in his Italian landscapes we see the indications of the wonderful effects of atmosphere which characterise his pictures when he has settled down into his permanent manner—has found his own individuality. One day an art critic was praising the lightness of Corot's foliage. "Yes," said he, "the birds must be able to fly through the branches." He was essentially an outdoor artist, saturating himself with Nature in all her varied aspects, and transferring her to canvas in all her ever-changing moods.

He has himself given to us, in a letter to

a friend, an almost autobiographical description of his own relations with the outdoor world, and so beautiful is his description, so greatly does it help us to understand his work, that we quote it almost in full, although we know that many of our readers will have seen it often before.

"A landscape painter has a delightful day. He gets up about three a.m., before sunrise. He goes and sits down under a tree, and waits, watching.

"At first there is little to be seen. Nature lies behind a white veil, through which some vague masses are faintly visible. Everything is sweetly scented, and trembles under the wakening breeze of the dawn.

"*Bing!* The sun gets clearer and begins to break through the fine veil, behind which shelter the fields, the woods, the distant hills. The mists of night still lie like silver on the cool grass.

"*Bing! bing!* First one ray of sunlight— then another. The flowerets awake, each one bathing in its drop of pearly dew. The leaves stir in the chill morning air. The birds begin to twitter their morning prayer. One sees nothing, yet all is there!

"The landscape is hidden as yet behind the

ENVIRONS DE ROME, 1866

transparency of the mist, which will gradually be absorbed by the sun, and as it rises we see the silver river, the meadows, the cottages, the ever-receding horizon. At last we can see what at first we could only guess at. *Bam!* The sun has risen. *Bam!* A peasant crosses the end of the field with his cart and oxen. *Ding! ding!* says the bell of the ram who leads the flock. *Bam!* Everything sparkles, glitters ; all is in full light, still, soft, and caressing . . . and I paint ! I paint !

"The far distance in its simple contour and harmony fades into the sky, through an atmosphere of mist and ether. The flowers raise their heads, the birds flit to and fro. A peasant riding a white horse disappears down the narrow path. And the artist ? He paints !

"Ah ! the beautiful dun-coloured cow, chest deep in the moist grass. I will paint her. *Crac!* There she is ! Capital ! What a portrait !

"*Boum! boum!* The sun begins to scorch. All grows heavy and dull. The flowers droop, the birds are silent ; only sounds from the village reach us. It is the blacksmith, whose heavy hammer strikes the anvil.

"*Boum!* Let us go. We see too much. There is nothing left to the imagination. Let

D

us go to breakfast at the farm. Work, my friends! I will rest! I will doze and dream of my morning scene. I will dream of my picture, and later on I will paint my dream."

The letter is too good to condense, but our pages are too few to give it in its entirety; here, however, is the end :—

"*Bam! bam!* The sun descends towards the horizon, it is time to return to work.

"*Bam! bam!* The sun is still sinking in an expanse of orange and gold, fiery-red and purple—ah! that is pretentious and vulgar, I will not have it. We will wait, we will seat ourselves under the poplar near the pond, smooth as a mirror.

"Nature is tired, but the little flowers are still gay. Little, little flowers! they are not like men who complain of everything. They have the sun on their left—they have patience to wait. 'It is well,' they say; 'soon we shall have our desire'—they are thirsty, but they wait. They know that the spirit of the dusk will bring them dew sprinkled from invisible fountains; they keep their patience and they praise God.

"But the sun sinks yet lower towards the horizon.

"*Bam!* His last ray, one which edges the

flying clouds with purple and gold. Now it is gone. Good, dusk is at hand. Heavens! what charm!

"The sun has sunk. There remains but a soft filmy touch of pale yellow—the last gleam from the sun which has dropped into the deep blue of night—melting from soft green into a yet paler turquoise of an intangible delicacy and an indescribable liquid mistiness. The fields lose their colour, the trees stand out in grey or brown masses, the dark waters reflect the clear colours of the sky. Everything is fast fading, yet we know that everything is still there. All is vague, confused, for Nature is falling asleep. Yet the fresh evening breeze whispers in the leaves, the voices of the birds and the flowers are raised in prayer, the dew-drops pearl upon the grass.

"*Bing!* A star plunges into the water. Beautiful star, whose twinkling the shimmering of the water augments a hundredfold, you smile on me, and your own eyes brighten as you flash on me.

"*Bing!* A second star shows in the water, a second eye is opened; welcome, bright and shining stars!

"*Bing! bing! bing!* Three, six, twenty stars! All the stars of the sky have their

meeting-place in this happy pool. All is dark
—the pond alone shines out of the darkness, a
abyrinth of stars.

"The illusion is over. The sun having gone
to rest, the inner sun—the sun of the soul—
the sun of art—arises. Good! my picture is
finished."

Here we see the artist, the poet, the lover of
nature; we see also the man who, as we have
already said, never painted nature in a convulsion. When the sun blazes at full midday,
when it sets in an orgy of colour, Corot will
have none of it; he makes no attempt to catch
even a fleeting impression of its glories: "I
will rest," he says; "I will go sit by the
pond until Nature returns to her more peaceful
moods."

But in her peaceful moods Corot never
wearied of studying her, and of teaching
others to study her. "If," he used to say to
his pupils, "God does not speak to you in the
face of nature, it means that your hour is not
yet come, or that you have mistaken your road;
if the latter, then go and seek elsewhere." It
will be interesting to print here Albert Wolff's
account of the artist as he appeared to his
friends when an old man of seventy, still striving to learn some secret yet unrevealed.

"Some eight or nine years ago," Wolff writes in 1880,* "in the beautiful summer days, one might see at Ville d'Avray one of the most touching spectacles ever presented by an artist. It was that of an old man, nearly arrived at the end, dressed in a blouse, sheltered by a cotton umbrella, observing nature like a young student, seeking to surprise some secret still undiscovered in spite of his seventy years ; smiling at the twittering of the birds and occasionally responding with a bar or two of some gay song and the light-heartedness of twenty years.

"Old as he was, he still sought to learn. For over half a century he had contemplated nature, believing that to master his art was an impossibility, and feeling that one human lifetime, however long, was not long enough in which to learn all the infinite variations on the face of Nature.

"This old man, one of France's greatest painters, was named Jean Baptiste Corot. His fame, now unquestioned, was the result of fifty years of labour, the first half of which were spent in a continuous struggle against a still triumphant routine.

"No trace of these combats against conven-

* *Cent Chefs-d'œuvre des Collections Parisiennes.*

tionality was left upon Corot's soul, and in the many interviews I had with the fine old artist in his later years no accent of bitterness or resentment was discernible in him against the blind prejudice which had passed by his canvases unmoved and unconvinced.

"Occasionally he could be heard talking to himself and exclaiming, 'That's famous!' or 'That will have to be done again, lad.'

"One looked upon Corot with the tender admiration due to this beautiful old age. In order to explain the delightful freshness of his ideas we must remember that he had always been a spoilt child of Nature. The comfortable circumstances of his parents and the allowance this enabled them to make their artist son gave him the opportunity of devoting his whole life to his art, unhampered by the sordid details of an everyday struggle with poverty."

But to go back to 1847, when we left our artist with his first purchaser. About this purchase a characteristic story is told that when congratulated by his friends on the sale, Corot replied sadly, "Yes—but now my own collection is incomplete!" It was in 1847, too, that Corot received the decoration of the Legion of Honour.

The year 1848 was an important one for Corot.

LA ROUTE D'ARRAS

Up to this date there had been no Hanging
Committee for the Salon, but the selection of
pictures had been made by the members of the
Academy of France, many of whom were not
artists at all, and yet acted as sole judges.
This state of things had naturally resulted in
the rejection by the Salon of the work of most
of the pioneers of the day, and some of these,
disgusted at the ignorance thus shown, had
ceased to send in pictures at all. Now all was
changed. A system was introduced by means
of which fifteen judges were elected by the
artists to form a "Jury of Selection," and
when the ballot was declared, Corot came out
ninth on the list.

This method of electing the jury has continued to be practically the same up to the
present day, and from 1848 to 1870 (when
he declined the honour, and was replaced
by Chaplin) Corot invariably formed one of
its members. In 1855, too, he was one of
the special jury of thirty-four appointed by
Napoleon III. for L'Exposition Universelle.

From 1848, whenever a Salon was held,
Corot was well represented in it, but so far off
still was the time when the public taste had
sufficiently ripened to appreciate him, that an
amusing anecdote comes to us from a later

Salon, probably about 1857. On the opening day he received a telegram from an unknown source, asking whether a certain picture of his was for sale, and if so, at what price? Corot in some excitement replied that the picture was for disposal for the sum of 10,000 francs.

Having despatched his answer, he tormented himself with doubts as to the wisdom of putting so high a price on his work, and made up his mind to hear nothing further of the inquiry. We can imagine his delighted surprise when in the course of a few hours he received a second telegram accepting the terms. So little success had he had hitherto, that he could not believe his own eyes. "What can have happened?" said he. "Did I by chance drop one nought?" So he re-telegraphed his price, this time in words instead of in figures, and was greatly relieved when informed that the inquirer still wished to purchase the picture at the price named.

There was no Salon in 1858, but Corot was persuaded, with some difficulty, to entrust thirty-eight of his pictures to an auctioneer, M. Boussalon, who had arranged for a public sale. Corot's works realised £570—a sum of which the auctioneer is said to have been ashamed, but which Corot thought almost too high to be believed in!

His studio was always full of pictures, and he parted with any one of them reluctantly, and many never left his rooms until the sale which took place after his death, and which comprised 931 finished works, sketches, and drawings. Besides these, there were also many unfinished canvases with the names of dealers or art patrons on the back. They had been ordered sometimes years before, but Corot never touched a canvas unless he felt inspired by that particular one. It is said that it was his custom when arriving at his studio in the morning to spread out his various half-finished works on the floor and study them, in order to find out which particular one suited his mood for the day.

Apropos of the number of his own paintings with which the artist was invariably surrounded, Robaut tells the following amusing story. A country connoisseur came to the studio to buy a picture. But when once inside he saw pictures everywhere, hanging on the walls, placed on easels, leaning against the legs of easels, and filling every corner. The would-be purchaser was aghast. "Why," he exclaimed,

"this is a manufactory!" and he departed
without making a purchase.

The story of another purchaser who also
ended by not obtaining a picture is told by
Dumesnil. An amateur collector, whose name
does not appear, had ordered a picture. Walking one evening towards twilight from Versailles
to Ville d'Avray, Corot was seized with an
unusually keen sense of the beauty of the place
and the hour. Arrived at home he continued to
dream of the scene until it took definite form,
and on the following day he hastened back to
Paris to his studio (having, as we have seen,
none at Ville d'Avray) to paint a picture. The
inspiration was so strong that by the end of
the day the picture was finished. Great was
his own astonishment. "What," said he to
himself, "already finished! And I am to receive quite a large sum of money for the ex-
penditure of so short a space of time! That
must not be! Let's put more work into it;
and yet—to add may be to spoil; we will leave
it and study the skies through the smoke of a
pipe!"

The purchaser arrived, looked at the picture,
hesitated, and at length said, "Well, it's not
a very cheerful picture! I'll tell my wife about
it, and let you know what she says before decid-

ing." A few days later Corot received a note refusing the picture, because "from my description of it my wife finds it decidedly too dull." Corot accepted the result philosophically. "Someone else will have it, that's all," he told himself. And Diaz was that "someone," when a little later it was exhibited in the Boulevard des Italiens. Ten or twelve years after the date to which these stories belong Corot had become famous, and dealers were pressing for the execution of orders, and he then took a great delight in keeping them waiting. "Oh yes," he would say, "you will get your picture, but I'm sure I can't say when—you are entered in my order-book under 'number 328'!"

In 1862 there was again no Salon, but Corot sent a picture to the International Exhibition in London, but it did not attract much attention. We are told also that the artist himself visited England for a week during the summer of the Exhibition, and is said to have expressed surprise at seeing so much sunshine, for it was a warm, fine season, and he had been led to expect a foggy, rainy England.

The years 1863 to 1867 saw Corot represented at the Salon by two or three pictures each year, and there was some talk in the latter year of awarding him the *médaille d'honneur;* but for this he was in reality ineligible from not being a historical painter. 1867 brought him a personal grief in the death of his patron-friend and pupil, M. Dutilleux, with whom, after the first year of his mother's widowhood, he had become intimate, and with whom many of his little excursions in search of "subjects" were taken. The death of this friend was a great loss to him, for Corot was a firm friend, and after M. Dutilleux's death he apparently remained on intimate terms with his widow, to whom, in 1871, we find him writing the following characteristic letter :—

"VILLE D'AVRAY,
"*le 3 août,* 1871.

"MADAME ET AMIE,

"Je sors mes lunettes avec rapidité pour vous écrire que nous sommes installés, ma sœur et moi : la maison est nettoyée et les traces prussiennes ont disparu. Ma sœur est en assez bonne santé, elle m'a chargé de vous faire ses compliments ainsi qu'à toute la famille. J'ai commencé des études à Ville d'Avray, j'ai retrouvé des motifs, mais ce ne sont pas les jolis marais d'Arleux, Paluel, etc. Je pense que vous passez de jolis moments dans ces jolis bateaux et jolis bois du pont de Paluel et les jolis

EVENING LIGHT

Bois d'Oisy. Je me suis bien amusé là-bas et
je pense que vous en faites encore tout autant,
pour ne pas en perdre l'habitude et que Mme
Marie aura retrouvé du calme, du repos et alors
la santé. Je fais des prières pour que tout ça
se réalise.

> " Pêchez aussi de belles anguilles
> Sauce Moutarde
> Et au premier repas, je vous prie,
> Buvez à la santé du pauvre petit nègre,
> Votre nourrisson
> Pendant la Commune.
> J'ai l'air d'écrire en vers.

" Embrassez bien pour moi M. et Mme Alfred,
Mme Marie et Léontine. Mes amitiés à Charles,
à M. et Mme Seiter, à Paul et sa famille, et à
M. Pochez, quand vous les verrez.

" Recevez, Madame et amie,

" l'assurance de mon amitié,

" C. COROT.

" P.S.—Les études que j'ai rapportées ont
été goûtées et prises presque toutes."

The number of persons whom he mentions
by name give us some insight into Corot's
amiability of character. He had evidently
"made friends" with half the neighbourhood
at Arras.

In 1868, 1869, 1870 Salons were held, and at each of them Corot was represented by two or more pictures.

In 1870 the artist, already seventy-four years old, made an allusion to his age. He had always been noted for a fine physique, so much so that his friends used to say he would "live to be a hundred." "A hundred and four," he would answer. "I think *le bon Dieu* will grant me the extra four." And now, in the spring of 1870, the old man goes once more to Ville d'Avray "to rest himself with work." As he says: "I can't have more than thirty years left, and they go so fast! Seventy-four have already flown, and to me they seem to have gone as fast as the journeys one takes in one's dreams."

Only four of the "thirty" were left; but those were filled, as all the rest had been, with unceasing work and constant acts of sympathy and good-fellowship to those around him.

When he heard that the siege of Paris was inevitable he returned from Ville d'Avray, and remained there until the end, spending large sums of money in the relief of the poor and sick, and going himself about amongst the wounded. It is said that he gave as much as 25,000 francs (£1,000) for public use. He subscribed also largely towards the liberation of territory held by the Prussians, especially for the freeing of the land around his beloved Ville d'Avray. At the end of the war he was sent for by the mayor of his district and requested to receive back some 5,000 francs which had remained unused. "I can't take it back," said Corot. "My purse doesn't like having back again what has once gone out of it—besides, it upsets my accounts!" "Well," said the mayor, "shall I give it in your name to the technical school for boys?" "A capital idea," said Corot, and went away. In a few minutes, however, he was back again. "There must be no cause for jealousy, monsieur," he said. "You have doubtless a technical school for girls also. Here is a similar sum for that." His income at this time was about £8,000 a year.

After the siege was over Corot went off once more on a sketching tour, first to Arras and Douai, and then (after a brief return to Paris) to the north of France. From this visit he brought back four or five pictures.

The years 1871–74 were years of unremitting labour, the old man of seventy working with the ardour and freshness of youth.

In 1872 he went south, and was struck by

the extraordinary "greens" of the landscape. "Wait till I have taken it all in," he said; "then I'll show you something!"

In 1873 he exhibited "Le Passeur," and there was some talk of awarding him the *médaille d'honneur;* but now, as again in 1874, it was bestowed elsewhere.

But 1874, which emphasised in a special manner that persistent ignoring of Corot in which the Académie had so consistently persevered, saw also the greatest triumph of the master.

There appears to have been little doubt, even amongst the most sceptical, as to who would be the recipient of the gold medal, and its presentation to Corot was discussed with the utmost confidence. Imagine, therefore, the storm of indignation which was raised by the announcement that the honour had been again withheld. Everyone had regarded it as the right of the veteran landscape painter, now as popular in his native country as he had been neglected in his earlier days, and when, after the usual deliberation, the award was made to Gérôme, public indignation broke bounds, and the newspapers were not sparing of their remarks on the injustice of the act. It is said that Gérôme himself was fully sensible of the injustice, and was greatly tempted to refuse the honour, more especially as the pictures exhibited by him in that year's Salon, and upon the merits of which the award was ostensibly made, did not show his best work. His generous objections were, however, overruled by his father-in-law, M. Goupil, the head of the firm of art publishers of that name. Possibly his estimate of his son-in-law's gifts coincided with that of the jury, perchance he was moved by more personal considerations; apart, however, from the slight cast upon Corot by the preferment of Gérôme, the jury were free of all blame in the selection of this undoubtedly talented painter. But the art-loving public of France was aroused, and being powerless to annul the decision of the electoral body, they set themselves to devise a plan by which to give special honour to their neglected favourite. Meetings were held to discuss the matter, and committees were formed. At length it was resolved that a special gold medal should be struck and publicly presented to Corot in the name of his artist friends and admirers. A subscription list was opened, which by the end of November had reached the not inconsiderable sum of 4,000 francs (£160).

It is pleasant to read in the *Academy* of December, 1874, in a letter from P. Burty,

E

its Paris correspondent, that Englishmen responded promptly to the call to prove their admiration for one of the greatest of landscape painters. "We have already," writes P. Burty, "received remittances from England, with letters which increased their value tenfold. Your countrymen," he continues, "have recognised the fact that genius is an international inheritance. I hope that fresh subscribers will yet add their names to this list, which will be copied on parchment and presented to the aged master, and bequeathed to his family as a patent of nobility." We do not know what was the final result of this appeal as far as England was concerned, but we hope that our countrymen made a generous response to so flattering an invitation. No list of subscribers to the medal appears to have been published, but we have some details of the presentation committee. It was composed as follows :—M. Marcotte, an old friend of Corot, was president, and he was supported by Ch. Daubigny, Jules Dupré, H. Daumier (the caricaturist), Roybet, Ed. Frère, Alfred Stevens, and Philippe Burty.

On the reverse of the medal (the work of M. Geoffroy Dechaume) is a palette with a crown, a branch of laurel, and an inscription ; on the obverse the profile of the master.

But by the time the day for presentation (December 29th, 1874) arrived Corot's last illness had begun. In October, 1874, his sister, with whom he had shared the little house at Ville d'Avray for so many years, died, and from that moment his own health began to fail. At the presentation fête given in his honour at the Grand Hotel it was already noticed that he seemed weary and in pain. "Alas ! " says Dumesnil, " how he was changed ! The lines of his face told of suffering ; he spoke nervously and feverishly, yet with animation ; he stood all the time and made efforts too great for his strength." Nevertheless, it must have been a happy moment for him when, his health having been drunk amidst ringing cheers, he opened the little case presented to him by M. Marcotte and read the inscription :—

À COROT,
Ses Confrères et ses Admirateurs.
Juin, 1874.

" It is a happy thing," whispered the old artist to his friend, " to feel beloved like this."

During the next few weeks he prepared his pictures, " Biblis " and " Les Plaisirs du Soir," for the Salon, and paid a last visit to Ville d'Avray. The signature to his exhibits was placed on them by the artist when actually on his death-bed, and Dumesnil tells us that this was the last occasion on which his fingers held the brush.

On Tuesday, February 23rd, 1875, at half-past eleven at night, those fingers again moved as if still working at his beloved art. "Look!" he cried, "how lovely! I never saw such exquisite landscapes!" But those "exquisite landscapes" could never be transferred to canvas, for the artist who saw them was dead.

BATEAU SOUS LES SAULES

CHAPTER IV

FUNERAL—EXHIBITION—MEMORIALS

TWO days later, on February 25th, 1875, a funeral service was held at the church of Saint Eugène. The ceremony was very simple, but the coffin, on which were placed the cross of the Legion of Honour and the gold medal presented by his friends but two months before, passed through a crowd of some thousands of persons — a crowd filled with emotion and respect for the dead artist.

The music for the service was the Andante from Beethoven's Seventh Symphony, arranged as a requiem by M. Elwart, to whom Corot had once expressed a desire to be buried "to the sound of this sublime melody." The words were sung by the famous tenor Faure, who also was a friend of the artist.

After the solemn Mass the funeral cortège passed on to the cemetery of Père-la-Chaise. The pall-bearers were MM. Jules Dupré, Oudinot, Lavieille, and Charles Daubigny, all of whom claimed to be his friends and pupils. Arrived at the cemetery, a fine funeral oration was spoken by M. de Chennevières, Directeur des Beaux-Arts. But M. Roger-Milès in a sympathetic sketch of Corot, published in 1901, tells us of an unconscious tribute to Corot the man, of more worth, perhaps, than all the eulogies given to Corot the artist. Someone looking on at the funeral asked of a poor woman standing by, "Whose funeral is it?" "I don't know his name," she replied, "mais c'est un homme de bien." "Un homme de bien!" says M. Roger-Milès, "quelle meilleure parole pour résumer l'œuvre et la vie de Corot."

Immediately after his death Corot's friends, and amongst them might be counted all the artists of any reputation in France, decided to hold a posthumous exhibition of his work, and the following announcement appeared in large type in *l'Art* for April, 1875 :—

"Exposition de l'œuvre de Corot.

"Desiring to make the exhibition of Corot's works as complete as possible, the committee request all collectors who possess works by this master to communicate with the secretary of the committee, M. Edouard Daliphard, 18, Rue de la Glacière.

"Members of the committee have been appointed to inspect proffered loans in order to avoid the necessity of returning those which the dimensions of the Hall of Melpomene and the conditions of the exhibition might prevent them from accepting. The work of selection will begin on Monday, May 3rd.

"(Signed)
"The Secretaries of the Committee,
"E. Daliphard,
"O. Brillouin."

Then followed a list of names of subscribers and the amount subscribed by each to the monument which it was proposed to erect to Corot's memory. Glancing along the list, we see more than one name opposite the sum of half a franc, and we take it as a tribute to the memory both of the man and the artist that no one, however poor, desired to be left out of the movement.

· The catalogue—prefaced by a short notice of the artist by Philippe Burty—included some 225 works, and the exhibition took place on May 22nd at the Palais des Beaux-Arts.

Every effort had been made to ensure the collection being as complete as possible. Notices were published in all places where they would be likely to attract the attention of owners of Corot's pictures. In our own *Academy* for May 8th, 1875, we find a notice of the proposed exhibition and an appeal to English owners of "Corots" to lend their pictures in order to forward the desire of the committee to make it as representative as possible.

Writing afterwards in *l'Art*, M. Daliphard greatly regrets the absence of two of the master's chefs-d'œuvre. "One—'Le Chemin de l'Église de Marseilles'—was in the possession of a certain Mr. Y. Z., who refused to lend it on the ground that it would leave a vacant space on his walls at a season when he was in the habit of entertaining his friends! The second—'Macbeth'—belonged to Sir R. Wallace, who was unable to get at the picture, it being at that moment packed and warehoused." But although we cannot trace any English exhibits, we hope other owners were more generous.

The proceeds of the Exhibition and the money subscribed by Corot's friends and admirers were placed together and ultimately used to erect a monument to his memory, although this was not done until May, 1880, more than five years after his death.

The monument took the form of a white marble fountain placed by the side of the famous pond at Ville d'Avray, close to the artist's house. The bust of the artist, surrounded by a laurel wreath which forms the centre of the fountain, was carved by Geoffroy Dechaume, who, it will be remembered, had also designed the famous "medal." Here in front of the fountain, Coppée, in his character of "Corot's Nymphe," wrote his immortal verses—verses which in their simplicity are peculiarly fit to keep in our memories the image of the "goodman in the blouse":—

" Le bon Corot m'aimait, je suis l'une de celles,
   Alors que l'aube emplit de vagues étincelles
      L'horizon frileux du matin,
   Que l'artiste—c'était son heure favorite—
   Voyait passer, avec les yeux de Théocrite,
      Au fond du brouillard argentin.

    .   .   .   .   .

" Je le connaissais bien, le vieux bonhomme en blouse,
   Et quand il préparait sur un coin de pelouse
      Son chevalet et ses pinceaux,

    Pour embellir encor ses extases secrètes,
    J'étais là, j'exaltais l'odeur des violettes,
        J'excitais le chant des oiseaux.

    .   .   .   .   .

" Mais vous nous le rendez, voici notre poète !
    Un doux rossignol chante au-dessus de sa tête.
        C'est lui ! nous le reconnaissons !
    C'est bien son visage !   Il regarde, il respire !
    Oiseaux ! fleurs ! désormais vous le verrez sourire,
        Dans vos parfums, dans vos chansons ;

" Et près de la fontaine où vit sa chère image,
    Portant comme aujourd'hui quelque odorant hom-
        mage,
        Je reviendrai souvent m'asseoir
    Au moment qui berçait si mollement son rêve,
    Quand l'étang s'assombrit, et quand au ciel se lève,
        La divine étoile du soir !"

Corot, as we have said, left his work ready
for the Salon of 1875, where his three pictures
—"Les Bûcherons," "Plaisirs du Soir," and
"Biblis"—appeared hung with black crêpe.
Castagnary writing of them remarks that there
is nothing new, nothing unusual about them,
but that they show the old artist with as clear
an eye, as steady a hand, as fresh a fancy,
as keen a sensibility as ever. "Death," says
he, "might surely have had pity and have
paused before cutting short so sweet a life-
work." It will be interesting to note the
estimation in which Corot was held by the

world at the time of his death, in so far as we can do so by an examination of the prices paid for his pictures at the sales immediately following.

We read in the *Siècle* that on April 19th of the year of Corot's death there took place a sale of a private collection belonging to a certain Monsieur H——. This collection comprised, amongst other things, sixteen pictures by Corot. "What wealth!" says the *Siècle*. "Sixteen Corots, of which 'La Chaumière,' 'Les Dunes,' 'Les Bruyères,' 'Le Ruisseau,' may count as amongst the most exquisite and delicately original of all the master's works."

The pictures were valued beforehand by an expert and sold well, although they did not fetch quite the sum at which they had been estimated. We give both the valuations and the actual prices.

	Valuation. Francs.		Actual Price. Francs.
La Chaumière	7,000	...	8,000
Les Bruyères	6,000	...	5,900
Les Dunes	6,000	...	4,900
L'Allée verte	4,000	...	3,000
Marcoussy	6,000	...	5,000
L'Étang de Ville d'Avray	8,000	...	6,700
La Femme à la Fontaine	3,000	...	2,350
La Fillette	1,500	...	1,080
Le Ruisseau	10,000	...	6,000
Matin d'Été	6,000	...	5,500

	Valuation. Francs.		Actual Price. Francs.
La Route Blanche . .	6,000	...	4,350
Le Chemin de la Maison de Corot			
à la Ville d'Avray . .	10,000	...	9,000
Au Bord de l'Eau . .	5,000	...	4,000
Le Chemin de l'Église .	2,500	...	2,050
Madeleine Pénitente .	2,500	...	1,200

In this same sale there were also works by Chintreuil, Courbet, Daubigny, Delacroix, Dupré, Millet, and De Neuville.

Dupré's "Un Marais" was valued at 20,000 francs and fetched 12,500.

Millet's "Glaneuses" was valued at 15,000 francs and fetched 12,100.

And a work of De Neuville was valued at 25,000 francs and fetched 11,500.

Soon after the loan exhibition, which had been held at the Palais des Beaux-Arts, a three days' sale took place of all the paintings, studies, sketches, drawings, and etchings in Corot's studio. The auctioneers were Messieurs Boussalon et Baubigny; the judge for the pictures, Durand Ruel.

Only two of the artist's more important works were left in his studio at his death, and these were acquired by the Luxembourg. A portrait of himself was sent to the Uffizi Gallery at Florence by his family after his death.

The "Vente Corot" comprised 931 finished

works, some copies from old masters made by
the artist himself, a few bronzes by Barye, and
a collection of the works of contemporary
artists. The manner in which he became
possessor of some of these paintings of his
contemporaries is characteristic of the man.
Many a young and struggling artist would
come to him in a state of actual want and of
mental depression, on account of the slowness
of the buying public to appreciate his work.
Corot would take a picture in pawn, as it were,
and advance the much-needed money. "I shall
be the gainer by this transaction," he would
say, when he paid the artist and took the
picture, "for some day this work will be a mine
of wealth to me."

When the contents of his studio came to be
sold, 305,785 francs were realised from his own
works, whilst not quite one-third of this sum
resulted from the sale of his collection.

We place below a list, in chronological order,
of the most important of the works included in
the sale, together with the prices paid for them.

	1822 to 1824			Francs.
Vue prise à Narni .	.	.	.	2,300
Rome : Jardin Farnèse	.	.	.	2,750
Castle of St. Angelo, Rome	.	.	5,000
Monte Pincio	.	.	.	1,705
Naples .	.	.	.	1,400
Rivage d'Italie	.	.	.	1,850

Francs.

1829 to 1833

	Francs.
Paris, au pont de Change	3,480
Portico of Chartres Cathedral. (August, 1830)	1,900
Honfleur: the Quay	3,050
The Forum. (Larger picture from study in Louvre)	2,650
Castle and Bridge of St. Angelo. (A second picture taken from the first)	3,500
Bassin à Honfleur	1,500
The Jetty at Havre on a Rough Day	3,000
Trouville. (Sketch on wood)	2,020
Fontainebleau	1,030
Forest of Fontainebleau: the Gorge	1,800

1834

Vue de la Ville de Gênes	3,550
Another: with two monks	2,500
A Volterra	1,295
Another: with rocks	2,100
Florence: from the Boboli Garden	1,900
Interior of the Baptistery of San Marco	1,400
Venice: Gondola and Canal	1,650
Venice: Sta Maria della Salute, across the water	2,100
The Grand Canal, Venice	5,500
The Grand Canal, with the Campanile of St. Mark	3,500
Riva: Como	2,200
The Town and Lake of Como	1,650

1835 to 1842

Agar (1835)	3,500
A Genève	2,100

1843

A Tivoli: Villa d'Este	4,000
A Némi	1,500
Jeunes Filles au Bain	1,400

1844 to 1850

Francs.

A Semur, le Chemin de l'Eglise	.	.	.	1,700
Ville d'Avray : Corot and his Mother in the Garden	.	.	.	1,700

1851 to 1855

Aux Mabilliers. (Study for solitude)	.	.	1,990
Environs de Beauvais	.	.	.	2,080
Monk Reading	.	.	.	1,500
Saint Lo	.	.	.	2,000
La Rochelle. (A second picture)	.	.	1,600
Hollande, près Amsterdam	.	.	.	1,140
Hollande, près Rotterdam	.	.	.	5,600
On the Mantes Bridge	.	.	.	1,155
Château Thierry	.	.	.	2,055
Ville d'Avray : the Washerwomen. (Removed from Corot's salon there)	.	.	3,100
Girl painting : with a Dog near	.	.	422
Mother and Child	.	.	.	1,500

1856 to 1859

Près Cayeux	.	.	.	1,010
Les Dunes à Dunkerque	.	.	.	1,800
Eglise reflétée dans un canal	.	.	.	1,000
Le Secret	.	.	.	1,610
Dante	.	.	.	15,000
Beaune la Rollande	.	.	.	3,800

1860 to 1865.

Campagne boisée	.	.	.	1,030
Ville d'Avray	.	.	.	1,015
Saint Malo	.	.	.	1,400
A Mortefontaine	.	.	.	9,500
A Isigny : Study for the Bacchante	.	.	1,600
Girl seated	.	.	.	4,000

1866 to 1870.

		Francs.
Paysage composé	.	2,600
La Comédie . . .	.	1,005
Près Mortefontaine : Pêcheur à la ligne .	.	1,020
Paysage composé (another) . .	.	1,000
Paysage composé (another) . .	.	1,000

1870 to 1875.

		Francs.
Landscape, with Bathers . . .	.	4,100
Young Woman . . .	.	1,900
Young Bohemian . . .	.	2,150
Village by the Sea . . .	.	1,625
Solitude. (A second picture) . .	.	2,830
At Brunoy. (May, 1873) . .	.	5,800
At Brunoy (another) . .	.	2,600
At St. Nicholas . . .	.	4,550
Near Gisors . . .	.	1,220
At Limetz	.	1,600
Landscape with Ruins . .	.	2,300
Les Nantoniers . . .	.	3,505
A Turn of the River . .	.	2,295
Souvenir of the Meuse . .	.	2,000
Ville d'Avray : Behind Corot's House	.	2,250
St. Nicholas (another) . .	.	3,450
At Labuissière . . .	.	1,240
A Arleux du Nord . .	.	3,400
The Tower at Crécy . .	.	1,500
Landscape . . .	.	2,250
Landscape (another) . .	.	1,000
St. Nicholas. (A third picture) .	.	3,800
Crécy. (A larger picture) .	.	1,810
Landscape : Study for Hamlet .	.	2,930
Sens : Interior of the Cathedral .	.	6,000
Landscape . . .	.	1,800
Landscape (another) . .	.	2,700

LE PECHEUR

Of the remainder of the works offered, few fetched more than 400 or 500 francs, and many of them were the slightest of sketches, some even unfinished sketches.

Prices remained much the same for the next ten years, but in 1886 at a sale of pictures in New York one Corot, the " Ramasseurs de Bois," was bought for the Corcoran Gallery at Washington for 72,000 francs. After this prices went up, and amongst more recent sales we notice the following sums :—

	1900.	Francs.
Le Matin .	. . .	. 32,600
Le Soir .	. . .	. 34,000
Le Pécheur	. . .	. 44,500

	1901.	
Les Bergers .	. .	. 43,800
La Cour de la Ferme .	. .	. 23,000

1903.

Orphée et Eurydice 21,500 dollars (roughly 105,000 francs).

St. Sebastian 2,500 guineas (roughly 63,000 francs).

Confronted with such a mass of work, we cannot but ask ourselves the question : " Was Corot's work really monotonous; did he, or did he not, justify the accusation of monotony so often made ? "

M. Chesneau in one of his criticisms says :

F

"Whether they represent autumn or spring, morning, midday, or eve, the landscapes of M. Corot are dominated by a half-light, a twilight which disguises both definite form and colour, showing only contours which are vague and undecided. . . . For the classical tradition Corot has substituted a conventionality of another kind ; a manner entirely his own, but which, nevertheless, has its fault ; that of presenting as nature what is in reality nothing but the dreams of the artist himself."

On another occasion he writes : "Out of the inexhaustible variety of effects which nature presents to us in the course of the seasons and hours, M. Corot is sensible only of the veiled light of spring dawns and of moist twilights."

Commenting on this passage, M. Roger-Milès remarks : "One must acknowledge that within these very studied lines Chesneau has said nearly the whole truth about Corot ; he has, however, not ventured to formulate his criticisms in one word and accuse the master of monotony. We have not the same scruples. Yes, for those who pass pictures without stopping to look at them, who look without seeing them, to these the work of Corot must appear monotonous."

Did these critics, we wonder, ever see Corot's

"Convent on the Banks of the Adriatic"—that dream-like pile of imposing buildings in stone, standing majestic on the heights, dominating the surrounding slopes of olives, silhouetted against a deep blue sky and a yet bluer sea? The picture is bathed in golden sunlight: the air quivers with the heavy heat of a southern day. As we gaze we feel the languorous atmosphere with the redeeming breath of life wafted across from the Mediterranean. Where are the "undefined forms," the "vague outlines" so crudely summed up by M. Chesneau as invariable accompaniments of Corot's vision? Where the monotony of colours attributed to the artist's work by M. Roger-Milès? In this land spring dawns unveiled in all her beauty, and the clear tones of twilight give place to the night of a thousand eyes.

Now take another scene—a summer day. A view of the Seine, a small picture. Here we gasp in the pitiless glare of a July sun; the leaves hang heavy in the noonday heat; no breath of cooling wind stirs the depths of the neighbouring woods, parched in the clear light of noonday.

And here is a third canvas, rich with all the wealth of summer. It is early morning, probably August; quite still; the sun shines but palely, lighting to silver the heavy dews still lying thick on meadow and pasture. Nature is awake, though resting, gathering strength to meet the coming heat of the approaching day. The cattle are feeding in the long grass, and the groups of trees in the park-like extent of meadow stretch away until the rising ground hides from us the distance. Here is no mystery of dawn, such summer day is to be found in any part of the centre of Europe. And once more look. "The Town of Perpignan." The blue waters of the river are tossing and foaming under the arches of the bridge which crosses it; a pile of red roofs rise one above another on the hillside; on the quay is a row of green-shuttered houses, under whose verandahs the shadows lie cool and deep, and whose once white walls the sun has kissed into radiant tones of rose-colour and gold.

And now let us journey with Corot to Rome and visit the Coliseum, whose noble proportions show out in all their varying shades of red and grey and yellow against a clear pale sky. Gazing at these magnificent ruins of an age which has left its mark upon the present day in matters of more moment than architecture, we people the Forum with the gorgeous figures of the Romans of old, brought to our minds by

VUE DE TOSCANE

the spirit of sympathetic comprehension which Corot has felt and has known how to communicate to his drawing.

Finally but one more, last, but not least, of a series of pictures revealing the innermost beauties of the landscape they portray. Let us rest on the Pincio, here in the deep shadows of the ilex trees by the fountain, whose basin shows black against the white light of the sun in the sky. The air is quivering in the heat, but our eyes, although dazzled, turn eagerly to that crowning glory of modern Rome, the dome of St. Peter's. Straight in front of us it rises majestic, turning from rose-colour to purple or grey as the sunlight caresses it lingeringly on every side in turn, loath to withdraw its rays from beauty so insistent yet so unconscious, so cold yet so dominating.

Are these the works of a dreamer whose visions are the creation of his own brain, uninspired by the scene he looks on? If indeed it be so, may the future give us more of such artists, whose spirit leads us to see beauties hitherto unrevealed to us, whose work breathes such truth that our eyes, turning from the painted representation to Nature herself, seem to behold her anew, and draw the nearer to her for the belief.

As we turn from these landscapes our attention is caught and arrested by another study; the canvas is covered with shades of greenish grey; shall we call it monotonous? From out of this vague-toned background gaze the eyes of a young woman. Her complexion is sallow; her hair parted in the centre is of a nondescript brown; her hands lightly clasp her knees, clad in a grey-green gown; her eyes are of much the same hue as prevails over the whole canvas; they are fixed upon space, dreamy, unconscious. "Introspection." That is its title. Where lies its charm? In its simplicity: its truth. Half fascinated we gaze into the girl's unanswering eyes, and there we read her thoughts—vague, wondering, dissatisfied, half apathetic, half tragic. But are they her thoughts we read or our own reflected there? "What is life?" What does it tell us? Whither is it leading?

CHAPTER V

COROT THE MAN

WE are accustomed in studying the lives of artists, great and small, to expect the dramatic. We look out for hereditary influence, picturesque circumstances, compelling forces as the man's legitimate background, and when we reach the man himself we take it for granted that we shall find something unusual, the waywardness and eccentricities of genius, the strong elementary passions, the follies and weaknesses, the charm or the repulsion which go to make up the somewhat theatrically conventional idea of "an artist." And our expectations are often enough fulfilled. The "artist" has always been the spoilt child of the conventional world ; for him ordinary rules of life, of education, even of morality, are set aside ; his bonds must be of the lightest, his freedom of the broadest, and so, with externals made easy for him, with an inward feeling half instinct, half tradition, that he *is* above and outside all rule, life too often takes him into side-paths and byways of existence where the popular biographer will find it unedifying to follow.

But with Corot this was not so. As a man he has no life-story, except that which is written large over all his work—the life of a simple, kindly soul at one with Nature in her peaceful, pastoral moods, unstirred by her passions, content, as we have said, to let them roll by whilst he sits still and does not even try to catch an impression.

As a boy, we find him drudging away diligently at the very ordinary school to which he had been sent, never distinguishing himself either for good or evil, doing his work passably well, and taking such little pleasures as are offered him soberly and somewhat sadly. The long walks with his "guardian" on school holidays must have been dull enough, unless the boy had already learned to see in nature those wonderful pictures which he afterwards

SOUVENIR D'ITALIE

transferred to canvas. Home life must have
been duller still, for Corot had no brothers, and
the business house in the Rue du Bac, from
which the father was absent all day at his own
work, and the mother was engaged with her
laces and ribbons, her ruches and her hat-
shapes, could not have offered much of a
playground for Camille and his two sisters.
However, we can picture the children playing
on the pavements of the quays, picking up
scraps of life from the life around them, perhaps running in and out of the Louvre, which
stretched its long line of buildings not far away
from the home of the "Marchande de Modes."
That Corot, as a man, retained a very strong
affection for one of his sisters, Madame Sennegon, we know, for she shared his home up to
the time of her death, and the failure of his
own health dated from this. But we have no
anecdotes, no letters which tell us anything
about the boy as a boy, what games he played
with his sisters, whether he hectored them as
brothers do, whether he was their slave or their
tyrant. The latter it would be hard to imagine,
for Corot the man was always gentle, always
tender, and although we have but few glimpses
of his relationships with women, we cannot but
believe that a tenderness which was marked

even towards his fellow-men, must have been
doubled when expressed towards women.

That he was of no particular importance
in his home we have plenty of evidence.
Emmanuel Dammage tells a story of a dinner
at the Barbizon about 1867, at which both he
and Corot were present. Corot being the oldest
guest was served first, and received the wing of
a chicken. He laughingly disclaimed his right
to this "regal portion and regal honour," saying that since he had abandoned trade (now
nearly fifty years ago) his family had always
regarded him as of no importance, a man to be
served last and with a "drumstick." "Give
me that now," he said, "and don't start me
with bad habits!"

For the greater part of his life the world
treated him as an artist in much the same way
as his family treated him as a man; but with
regard to his art Corot was more sensitive
than he was with regard to his personal
position, and there is little doubt that he
suffered keenly from the neglect shown him
by the general public, the picture-dealers, and
those in authority at l'Institut. "Alas! I am
still in the Catacombs," he used to exclaim
despairingly, when year after year saw his
work amongst the worst hung at the salons

and exhibitions.   But once back in his studio, surrounded by the work which he loved so dearly, his sunny nature reasserted itself and he would cry—" But I have my art—that remains ! "

His attitude towards his own work seems to have been more that of a lover than of a critic. He thought humbly of himself, wondering that anyone should care to pay so much as 10,000 francs for one of his pictures, content to accept the judgment of his parents, who placed the engraver of one of his works above the artist himself, rarely, if ever, comparing himself with other artists, and then always to their advantage.   " Rousseau ? " he said.   " Ah, yes, he is an eagle, and I—I am a lark, who sings sweet songs among the light clouds of a grey day."   And when the world took him at his own valuation and passed him by we find no sign of bitterness, no throwing aside of the brush in despair, only a severe withdrawing of himself into himself, and a smiling acceptance of the verdict.

Once—it was at the Salon of 1851, the last held in the Louvre—we are told Corot deliberately set himself to find out what the general public would have to say to his work could their attention be drawn to it.   He had a landscape very badly hung in the entrance-hall, and most persons simply passed through without seeing it at all. Knowing that people are like sheep—where one goes another follows— Corot stopped opposite his own picture for a while in order to induce others to look at it. A young couple approached. "It seems to me that this isn't bad," said the young man; "there's something in it." "Oh, come along," said his companion, "it's frightful." "*Tiens!*" said Corot to himself, for he was fond of telling the tale, "it serves you right for wishing for the criticism of the public." This same picture afterwards sold for 12,000 francs, and the purchaser was so pleased at becoming possessed of it that he gave a fête in honour of the event.

Corot was not the man to force his work or his own view of it on the public : he gave the world what it demanded, and what was rejected he kept for his own pleasure. Jean Rousseau tells us that, going one day to his friend's studio, he found him engaged on a life-sized portrait of a woman. "What a virile and supple painting with which to have delighted the eyes of Velasquez or Goya!" he cried. "You will surely let the world see this?" "Do you think so?" replied Corot, with a

LE BAIN DE DIANE

sigh; "when it will not even pardon me my smallest figures!"

But "the love of Art is not a sickness from which one may be cured, it is a vocation, unconsciously listened to and irresistibly obeyed." And this was how it appeared to Corot. "It must be confessed," said he one day, "that if painting be a folly it is a sweet one. I defy anyone to find in me any of the traces of the cares, ambitions, or remorse that ravage the features of so many. Ought I not, therefore, to love the occupation which gives me health, happiness, and content?"

Yet for all his enthusiasm, Corot's attitude towards art as a profession was always one of practical common sense. Placed himself by happy circumstance above the necessity for turning his beloved work into the means of supplying his daily needs, he was always keen on saving others from the possibility of having thus to degrade their art. Many aspirants came to him to consult upon the advisability of taking up painting as a career. "Have you fifteen hundred *livres de rente*," Corot would ask, "to ensure your liberty? Can you dine off a hunk of bread as I have done many a time? I never found myself any the thinner for it the next morning, so it is not very dangerous—and at need I recommend it." If the aspirant chanced to be the son of wealthy parents, and told Corot so, he would reply, "So much the better, you can amuse yourself with painting."

Simplicity was the law of his own life. For years, as we have seen, he pursued his art under the greatest difficulties as to outward conveniences, content, in Paris, with the smallest of studios, and when living at Ville d'Avray with his parents never even attempting to have a studio on the spot, but laboriously walking to and fro to his Paris "flat" to record an impression. He was an incessant worker, arriving at his studio at eight a.m., and working there until, as he said, "*le bon Dieu* put his lamps out" at dusk. His midday meal, a light one, was taken on a ricketty table in the corner of the studio, and it was the drawer of this table which served him in later years as a bank— a bank from which he constantly supplied the wants of those less fortunate than himself. Of his tender-hearted benevolence endless stories are told, and this benevolence was so well known that it was often imposed upon. He himself tells us that his heart felt so light after a deed of charity that his work "went better," and that on these occasions he would sing as

he painted, adding words to his tune somewhat
in the following style : " Here we place a lit
—tle—boy—la-la-la, our lit—tle boy requires
a cap—there 'tis—there 'tis—la-la ! " and so on.

Corot had lived on so little for so many years
that even when he grew comparatively rich he
needed no money for his own pleasures. But
for a friend in need he would not hesitate to
spend even large sums.

Honoré Daumier had lived for years at
Valmondois in a small house, which he had
hoped to be able to purchase. Far from the
realisation of his hope, however, there came a
day when he was threatened with eviction.
Corot, hearing of the matter, hastened to the
spot, bought the property, paying cash down
for it, and gave the title-deeds to his friend.
"You are the only man in the world," said
Daumier, with emotion, "from whom I could
accept such a gift without a blush."

But Daumier was not the only well-known
name with which Corot's generosity is connected. Shortly before his death he was engaged in a large pecuniary transaction with a
certain dealer, and was due to receive some
thousands of francs. When the money was
being paid over to him, Corot placed aside
10,000 francs, and returned it to the dealer.

" Will you be so good," he said, "as to take this and pay every year for the next ten years a pension of 1,000 francs to Madame Millet, the widow of my friend ? "

Besides these and other celebrated recipients of his charity, there were endless acts of private benevolence, with some of which we are acquainted. The following story comes from a correspondent to the *Athenæum* about the time of the artist's death. One morning a dealer had come to pay Corot a small sum of 500 francs. Whilst they were talking, a woman with two children came in. She told a piteous tale of the illness of her husband, a model— they had no money and were starving. Corot said his purse was at home, he could give her nothing, and he pushed her gently towards the door. Arrived there, he pressed into her hand the 500 franc note just paid him by the dealer, explaining that *he had no change!* Another anecdote shows us how great was his dislike to being found out in his charitable acts. Some of his money was invested in house property, the management of which was entrusted to a relative. When rents were due and the tenants could not pay, they would come direct to their landlord, complaining that the manager was hard - hearted. " I can't listen to your complaints," Corot would say, "but here is the money to pay the rent; only whatever you do, don't say where it came from, or I shall get into terrible trouble!"

We can imagine that the calls on such generosity were endless, and that even Corot's patience sometimes failed. On one occasion he is said to have been "out of humour," perhaps from too great a demand upon his kindness, and to have denied a friend who asked for the modest sum of 5,000 francs. Scarcely, however, had the man left his studio when Corot was seized with remorse. He hurried to the famous drawer, took out a roll of notes, and hastening to his friend's studio, heartily abused himself and his "niggardly ways," and pressed on his friend an even larger sum than he had been asked for.

He was always ready to help; men and women, artists, friends and strangers, all came to him, and few went away without being benefited. He is said to have been always surrounded by admirers, chiefly young men who required his advice and assistance. Appian, Auguin, Ch. Boulogne, Chintreuil, Delpy, Dieterle, Daumier, L. Français, Flahant, Ch. Le Roux, La Vieille, La Croix, La Rochenoire, Lépine, Masure, Oudinot, Petitjean, and Servin,

G

all claim to have been his friends or pupils; but, as has been justly remarked, it was not difficult to assume a certain position of friendliness with a man of the easy-going nature and habits of Corot—to whom, indeed, up to a certain period in his career, anyone could gain access. For many years Corot's studio was invaded at all hours and by all sorts of people; but one year he was ill and advised by his doctor to lead a quieter life, after which access was not so easy. Appointments had to be made, and the concierge was told only to let in such visitors as he had orders to admit. This plan had some advantages, not the least of which to the visitor was that he really had the opportunity of some conversation with the master alone.

Of this later period an amusing anecdote is told. A certain friend of the painter's wrote to ask for an interview and permission to bring with him a visitor, a priest of some standing in the Church and an admirer of the artist. Corot replied fixing Thursday, as on Wednesday he had a model for the nude. The friend lost the note, got confused as to the days, and presented himself with M. the Abbé on Wednesday. The sitting was fortunately over and the model in faultless attire, but the picture was yet on the easel. The Abbé advanced and stood before it. Corot, in great confusion, swore under his breath at his friend's carelessness. "Monsieur," said the priest, "when I see some pictures of this kind at the exhibitions I turn away horrified at the thoughts they suggest, but this one makes me dream of heaven." "Ah, monsieur," cried Corot, in great relief and thankfulness, "you are a true artist as well as a man." This purity of feeling is characteristic of Corot, and was closely connected with the purity of his life. An intimate friend, writing in 1889, says of him: "Corot was purity itself. He had never any mistress but one—a true, great mistress, an idol visible and palpable to all. From her he received, even from his earliest youth, all his purity, his chastity, his passionate attachment to nobleness and virtue. You know her as well as I—she is Dame Nature."

To mankind Corot remained supremely indifferent. His kind and gentle nature was torn by any story of physical suffering, and he hastened to relieve any distress brought directly to his notice; but of humanity at large he knew nothing and cared nothing. His imagination, so keenly alive to the beauties and even commonplaces of inanimate nature, saw nothing in a

human being but a figure which might lend
a happy finish to a woodland scene, a peasant
who would add the necessary touch to enliven a
landscape. Shall we confess that herein for us
lies Corot's weakness? Herein lies the lack
which in front of the most exquisite of his canvases leaves us cold. Where is the touch of
passion which carries with it its own pardon in
the face of many faults? Where is the string
of hope, where the beacon lighting to fresh
effort in the face of many failures? Corot's art
is great, but that touch of humanity which
kindles life to meet life, that splendid spark of
immortality which raises Art above the mere
expression of the Beautiful, that we miss.
Corot's art is great, but it is narrow. In so
far as trees, skies, water, pastureland are universal, in so far is his art universal; but the
inner teachings of life he ignores. Suffering,
strife, decay, death, he will have none of them.
Yet it is through these that a higher existence,
a new life is attained. From the passing of
autumn the spring is born. But with the facts
of life Corot has no concern; he sees, enjoys,
and reproduces the moment, above all, the
moment which is beautiful or which veils in
mist all that might mar the beauty. Beauty is
of many kinds, and that is not the highest

MORNING

which bears no trace of the process through which it was evolved.

Of Corot's absorption in his work and his detachment from the affairs of the world around him there are many stories. To politics he was almost entirely indifferent. His days of activity were passed in the gayest and most modern of cities, that Paris to which he invariably returned when ready "to paint his dreams"; and yet, in the midst of its teeming population, at a time when life was so vivid in France, through its political uprisings, its tumults, its triumphs, its vicissitudes, Corot went on his way as undisturbed in his personal habits as if he were still buried in the rural district near Semur in which his forefathers passed an uneventful existence in field labour. The revolution of 1848, which for a time caused the upheaval of all Europe, passed him by; and when Louis Philippe, forced to fly, had with difficulty escaped with life and limb, Corot, hearing the fact from a visitor to his studio, remarked, "It would appear, then, that there are some people who are discontented!" Of the Coup d'Etat (December, 1851) he only became aware two months after it had taken place, and when informed of it by a friend he confessed that he had been so busy painting that he had not opened a newspaper for three months. Of literature the artist was almost as ignorant as of politics. It is said that on one occasion, hearing Victor Hugo's name mentioned, he remarked, "It would seem, then, that Victor Hugo is a man well known in literature." He used occasionally to buy books at the old stalls on the Quay, but it was for their shape or colour, not for their literary contents. He was no reader, the only work he was ever known to study being Corneille's tragedy of *Polyeucte*, and that he was still reading at the end of twenty years. As each year came by, he would say, "Now this year I really must finish *Polyeucte*"; but he never reached the end!

Of his own estimate of his work it is difficult to speak; that he loved every canvas he ever touched we have abundant evidence. Montrosier tells us how he found himself one summer evening with Corot almost alone in the Durand Ruel Galleries, where two of the latter's works were on exhibit. Corot walked round slowly, saluting the masterpieces collected there, and expressing his admiration in vivid ejaculations and exquisitely chosen words of criticism. When, as would occasionally happen, words failed him altogether, he would turn to Montrosier and press his hand, saying,

"C'est du nanon, ça cher ami." When he came to his own pictures, "Sodom" and "Macbeth," his face lighted up as at sight of a friend long missed; then turning away with tears in his eyes, he murmured, "Good-bye, my children," and walked to another part of the gallery to forget the parting he had just suffered.

On another occasion an alarmist friend asked him if his studio were insured, pointing out to him that he would sustain a loss of some 40,000 francs should his pictures be burnt, and emphasising his remarks by the story of the destruction by fire of the valuable collection of an acquaintance. "He didn't paint them!" interrupted Corot. "What did it matter? But I—I should die if such a thing happened to me."

Clarétie gives an anecdote which shows us, however, that Corot's affection for his own work was not that of ignorance, for he was perfectly aware of its artistic value. During the Franco-Prussian War a friend visited his studio, and the talk fell on the war and its leaders. "This little picture," said the artist, pointing to a small canvas, "this will last as long as any of Bismarck's work—moreover, it will have harmed no one." He was generous with his work, gladly lending it for exhibition, and on more than one occasion presenting specimens of it to public collections, but in later life he was as well aware of its pecuniary as of its artistic value. "I can give away a picture," he would say, "but I will not degrade my art by putting too low a price upon it."

We have tried to give in words some idea of the simple, tender, kindly human nature underlying the outward characteristics of Corot the artist. As it is always interesting to see how far a man's inward character is expressed in his personal appearance, let us examine the portraits to which we have access, and see how much of the man is visible in his physical presentment.

The best-known portraits in oil are one by Decan, exhibited in the Salon of 1875, another by Benedict Masson, yet another by Belly, and a fourth by the artist himself, which was presented after his death to the Uffizi collection of "Painters portrayed by themselves." Of black and white portraits there is a famous one, "Corot with his Pipe," by Gabriel Bocourt, etched especially for *l'Art*. It is perhaps the most vivid of all existing portraits, and gives the artist in his most wide-awake mood, puffing at his well-beloved pipe, which was always called in to help in his moments of inspiration. Another, by A. Gilbert (made by him from a photograph, and engraved by Perrichon), shows the artist in a dreamy mood, looking at the spectator, but with eyes reflecting thoughts in his own mind, and unconscious of what is taking place before them.

All these are taken in later life when the artist's hair was whitened by advancing age and his face lined with the experiences of life.

An engraving by B. Masson (1840) shows us the master at an earlier age, though even then by no means in his first youth, and is distinguished from most of the others by its giving the artist short hair. One other portrait with short hair we notice in a pencil sketch by his friend Français. Two other pencil sketches were made by Aimé Millet, one full face and one in profile. Photographs exist in abundance, and all more or less show the same characteristics.

The hair is abundant, probably coarse, and is allowed to take its own way as to arrangement, showing little sign of brush and comb or mirror. The face is square—the forehead particularly so — and the features thick and somewhat heavy. But the eyes are keen and

look you straight in the face, and the lines
round them are lines of humour and kindly
interest. The mouth, too, is firm yet tender,
and the whole face, though scored with the
lines of age, is strangely free from any marks
of passion or selfishness. Corot's was essentially a sunny nature, and the sunshine of his
life is reflected in his face as we see it in old
age—an old age of mellow ripeness without a
sign of decay. Corot was no humorist, yet
had some reputation for wit, and this together
with his simplicity and general kindliness made
him all his life through the centre of many
friendships—friendships which compensated
him for the neglect of the outside world during
the greater part of his life. A study of his
portraits helps us to understand his personal
charm; it helps us to understand, too, the
difficulty felt by other artists who on first
seeing Corot were unable to reconcile his un-
romantic appearance with his work. Clarétie
gives us a very good idea of the impression
made on a stranger by the artist's commonplace exterior in a description he gives of a
first sight of him at a theatre. For a moment
the impression made was one of an extremely
countrified appearance, but almost instantly
something on the stage caused his face to light

NOON

up, and immediately the peasant was transformed into the artist. The same writer goes on to a more minute description. "His head was powerful, his forehead grand, nevertheless his features were refined; a straight nose, drawn with one stroke; the mouth, which had the appearance of smiling willingly, was usually slightly open as that of one who is in contemplation; but that which struck one most was the forehead, that noble forehead crowned with a wealth of flowing hair. The whole countenance breathed two elements — gaiety and thoughtfulness. Lips that smiled, eyes that dreamed."

We have another personal account from Dumesnil, who, in his *Souvenirs-intimes*, says: "Corot was fairly tall and stout, of a robust constitution, and air at once vigorous, frank, and healthful; his eyes soft, yet bright; an expression of good-fellowship tempered by much tact, a great nobility in his whole appearance. These are the chief characteristics of the sympathetic personality of Corot. He had blue eyes, a high colour, and a complexion which gave him the look of a vine-grower of Bourgogne."

These rustic characteristics were partly due to his out-of-door life, for Corot was essentially an open-air artist, but it was partly due also to heredity. We know nothing of his mother or of the surroundings from which she sprang, but Corot *aîné* came of a family of Burgundian peasants. His grandfather (Camille's great-grandfather) had been a small farmer; his son became a barber, and his son again (Camille's father) ended by being a shopkeeper, although at one time holding some municipal post. Camille, however, born in Paris and of the bourgeois class—a class concerning itself mainly with the details of everyday life, ignoring alike both the past and the future—was essentially a peasant, and a peasant he remained to the end of his days. In his walks abroad he wore a long black coat and a high black satin stock; but when it was possible to ignore convention, when he desired to be completely at his ease, his instinct led him to adopt the costume of his class—a blue blouse and a cotton cap.

But of the man Corot there is little more to say—we must pass on to Corot the artist. We will do so in the words of Dupré: "As a painter we might replace him with difficulty, as a man—*never.*"

CHAPTER VI

COROT THE ARTIST

Simplicity of character shown in his work—Variety in work—
Architecture—Open-air studies—Freshness of vision and
reproduction—Love of Nature in her peaceful moods—
The "Towing-path"—Influence of early teaching—
Hard touch—Flat colour—Jal's criticism—Millais'
opinion—Nature's elusiveness—Four essentials for a
painter—Number of paintings in a year—Figures—
Flesh tints—The classical style—Chesneau on classical
landscape—"Hamlet"—The "Destruction of Sodom"
—Alfred de Musset and the "Etoile du Soir"—
Decorative painting.

WITH work so manifold in its branches,
so varied in character, it is indeed a
matter of some difficulty to decide of which
particular style to treat first. The very simplicity of Corot's character helped largely in
making him so many-sided in his work. In
classical landscape, in landscape as nature
presents it, in the imaginative, the rural, in
architecture, in figure painting, Corot was a
master ; each in its turn he made his own, and
in each he excelled. But great as he was, the

consciousness of his own power was never a factor in Corot's art. He had no theories, he made no attempt to attune Nature to his moods, he followed hers ; and herein lies one of the secrets of his greatness. There is no desire to force " Corot the painter " into the picture. In one hundred of his paintings we find one hundred painters ; for Corot, at the moment of painting, is just the man that the scene and the hour combine to make him.

" In Italy," wrote Corot in 1825, " the necessity for architectural drawing is so great that I must set myself to work to learn it." It is interesting to trace his steps upward through this special branch of his art. Of slight pencil sketches Corot unfortunately left but few from which we may gather his methods of study. One of the earliest efforts in architecture of which we know bears the date 1826, and is a painting of a portion of Rome in the neighbourhood of the Tombs of the Cæsars. We are struck with the amount of detail in the picture, and while from the artistic standpoint we are disposed to condemn, we cannot but see and admire in it the perseverance of the artist who, with his ideals always urging him towards the poetic treatment of a subject, yet for the sake of what he considered a necessity, constrained himself to mastery through hard work and study. This picture was painted during the period when his comrades refused to regard Corot as a serious student; and in truth an immeasurable distance lies between this sketch and the famous one of the Coliseum presented in later years to the Louvre. In point of time a few months only separate this laborious and heavy painting from the drawing of the Coliseum, endowed with the romance of a poet, and executed with the skill of an architect; and we marvel at the rapidity with which Corot attained such mastery of what had been to him but so short a time before almost a new art.

In the early days Corot painted entirely out of doors, and Clarétie speaks of a sketch which the painter himself pointed out to him as his first, representing merely the dead trunk of a tree, but holding promise of what the artist would attain to. It was dated 1822. After a while, however, Corot realised that the real object to aim at was to catch an impression, not to copy accurately what he saw; he therefore, while continuing to make careful studies, made also many notes for pictures to be afterwards completed in the studio. "You may cram more waves into the square inch than any other man of your age," wrote R. A. M. Stevenson ; "but it looks beggarly—reality being infinite—to count out hundreds when you might conjure up the illusion of millions." Compare this passage with Corot's own words : "If you crowd in too much you weaken effect, or falsify everything in the effort to be too exact," he says. "No two hours of the day are just alike, and you cannot put both on one canvas."

Dumesnil considers that the "classic was quite as much Corot's natural style as any other"; but if it be true that his natural bent lay in this direction, his genius leaned certainly towards the portrayal of nature, simple and unadorned. Like many another artist, Corot was not aware in what division of his art he stood pre-eminent. We have indeed to thank his inborn talent for much of his best work. When his genius burned strong and impelling within him he arose, took his tools, and wandering out, sat himself down, by preference where there were trees and some water, but with little definite choice of spot, and gave to the world the living reproduction of the atmosphere, the verdure, the life that surround us everywhere. In reality many of the sites immortalised by him have no merit of their own ;

EVENING

the scenery around Ville d'Avray is commonplace in the extreme, but with the magic
imparted to them on canvas, the glowing
freshness of spring with its eternal promise of
renewal, the lingering beauties and mysteries
of the fading autumn tints, are all borne in
upon us anew with every glance we take at one
of Corot's paintings. That quality which in
nature calls us to rejoice, makes our hearts
beat with the gladness of mere existence, that
is there. We stand before his pictures and
drink in their beauty, and as we turn away we
feel that we have inhaled a breath of pure air;
we have taken in new hope and new vigour;
we move away once more aware of the glory
of life, and awake to the possibilities which lie
before us.

For Corot was essentially a nature lover.
We see a summer sketch; we languish in the
heavy sensuous heat of a drowsy midsummer
day. "This," we say, "must be Corot's
favourite season!" And yet—what is this picture of autumn? the final glories of summer
burning themselves out in a passion of crimson
and orange; or this—which, indeed, appealed
more strongly to the artist, who regarded vivid
colour in nature as discordant—where the
passion has sunk to rest in the peace of a still

H

autumn evening, dreaming in perfect quiet till
the touch of spring shall awaken it to new life
and fresh beauty, shall call forth a fairy-like
green unsullied by the dust of the earth : pure,
unconscious as yet of the fuller fruition of
approaching summer.

Corot's soul is at one with the landscape,
and be the season what it may, of the North or
of the South, he is of the land and the hour
which he is painting.

Corot complained once to Daubigny that he
had no *métier*. "No *métier*," replied Daubigny ; "you put nothing on the canvas, yet all
is there." And so indeed it is. There is a
little picture, one of his masterpieces, called the
"Towing-path." Upon this work alone (the
canvas measuring less than a foot either way)
a whole treatise on painting might be written.
Of design there is little, of work less ; yet a
more consummate piece of art it would be difficult to find. Here is a description of the picture.
The bend of a river, probably the Seine, at a
most unattractive spot, entirely commonplace
and featureless. A flat grass path lies on the
right, and a white cart-horse with a lad on its
back plods along ; both common enough figures
at the side of any towing-path ; a line of trees
in a bluish distance, and a nearer group to the

left on the opposite bank of the river. So little paint that you could scarcely stain a palette knife with it if you scraped it all off the cloth, and yet what beauty, what harmony in the whole of these insignificant details! We have all passed such a spot a score of times and seen it in exactly this aspect, but it had no beauty then; it is the soul of the artist which has drawn that out—which has created a wonder; though we, seeing it, may learn to discover similar beauties for ourselves, and learning a lesson from Corot, evolve a world of delight out of a commonplace reality.

But Corot's habit of disregarding his own individuality had also its drawback. Had he not been so willing to learn from any and every possible teacher, he might the earlier have reached the summit of his power. In dozens of the small sketches which he made can be traced the combat of his desires with the result of the teaching he had received; and in many cases the battle was drawn and there is no victory to record for either side. We have seen a "Village Street," and a meadow with willows and water, and a small picture of "Geneva," of which we are almost tempted to regret the continued existence. Fortunately, nothing can detract from the real greatness

of the master, and these little daubs are,
perhaps, unworthy of mention; indeed, had
they by a fraction more nearly resembled the
master's best work, we might have condemned
them as spurious, but as it is, we are unable
to credit anyone but Corot himself with the
audacity of signing his name to the canvases.
There was a period when Corot must have been
under a strongly malevolent influence.   We
get, at this time, paintings so hard in touch
that it seems incredible that they came from
the same brush as "Le Patûrage," "Autumn,"
"An Evening Walk," and numbers of others.
There are some in which the usually unerring
sense of light and colour went entirely astray;
opaque browns and dirty greens predominate,
and the translucent quality which we look for
in Corot's best work is entirely absent.   These
paintings, which are mostly undated, were
doubtless executed about the early thirties,
when Jal, while classing Corot with Edward
Bertin and Aligny, complained that his colour
was flat and uninteresting.   Discouraging as
so adverse a criticism must have been to the
young painter, it was the first public notice
of any kind that his work received, and on this
account appeared to him as so decided a step
forward that he was the less inclined to quarrel

with the substance of it. Yet even in this transition period he often broke through the clouds among which he was struggling, and two of his early works, which are in their several ways unique, well deserve special mention.

We have an avenue of trees, with branches interlacing across a road, letting through splashes of bright sunshine upon it. There is a vigour in its detail that has an attraction entirely its own, and bears strangely little relationship to Corot's more developed manner. The picture may be described as a statement of fact without comment from its chronicler. A touch of red gleams from a petticoat in a sombre distance, and the flecks of light and occasional indication of single leaves among the wealth of greenery overhead reveal the earliest awakenings in Corot's mind of his later convictions.

The other picture contains detail minute enough to be worthy of the early Dutch school. We may classify the work as that of the "*style champêtre*." In the centre is a group of trees, upon which one may easily count the leaves, although they are revelling in the full luxuriance of midsummer ; to the left lies a careful stretch of meadow, some moments' study of which

might easily serve as a lesson to a youthful
botanist, so carefully is the natural growth
reproduced.   In the foreground is a pond, upon
the border of which a boat is just being prepared for a trip ; various women's figures—
peasants in red skirts—are disposed about the
picture, and from a sort of Italian opera gipsy
encampment under the trees rises the blue
smoke of a camp fire.   There is more paint on
this canvas than would in his later years have
served Corot for half a dozen pictures, nor
indeed would he then have found any use for
the rich red browns and emerald greens with
which this one abounds.   But the work has
merit; and it is said that one day Sir John
Millais, having spent some time in careful study
of its detail, expressed a full understanding of
the height to which its author had risen, "such
having been his beginning."

But Corot was rarely satisfied with his own
landscapes.   Nature appeared to him always
elusive.   " When I am in the fields," he said,
" I am seized with a rage against my pictures."

He describes also his difficulties with fast-
moving clouds.   " ' Stop ! ' said I, trying to
emulate Joshua with the sun.   But the clouds
continued to drive, the sky changing constantly

NIGHT

both in form and colour. I cried out to them to stand, if only for a moment, that I might not paint them wrongly—as though a sky standing still would be a sky at all!" Corot considered the highest compliment had been paid to him when a connoisseur in art told him that his clouds " moved well."

" There are four essentials for a painter," the artist used to say to the pupils who came to him in such numbers ; " form, colour, sentiment, and execution. Apply yourself to the acquisition of that in which you fail ; but above all obey your own instincts, your own individual method of looking at things. Leave all the rest, it does not matter. Be conscientious—the whole of Art lies in that."

Corot was a most prolific painter. Charles Bigot tells us that his friends estimated the number of his works at from four to five thousand ; and Corot himself told one of his friends that he painted about ten figure pictures a year. "This," he remarked, "mounts up in fifty years." And we know that he received so little encouragement in this branch of his art that it was by no means the one to which he directed his greatest energy. Rousseau was, however, a great admirer of Corot's figure paintings.

"I may be biassed," he remarks, "but to my mind Corot made advances on the art of his day which included advances on all that had gone before. He introduced the painting of the figure out of doors, a thing which even Rubens and Van Dyck had not attempted. Corot's flesh-tints are those of life, and if the drawing is not very studied in its detail, it is profoundly true in character and in general construction, and from this point of view, therefore, ranks with the greatest."

And yet his more highly finished works were almost entirely figure pictures of the classical sort, and this it is, doubtless, which has led some of his critics to consider that his talent lay as much in this direction as in landscape. Dumesnil remarks that if at the end of his career he devoted himself almost entirely to the creation of graceful and feathery landscapes, "it was perhaps more from the tendency of old age to renew the impressions of youth than from any other reason, for Corot never entirely abandoned compositions of a serious nature."

There is a note of regret over the neglect of classical work in these remarks which we find it hard to account for. Fine as were some of Corot's efforts in this direction, they are, like much of the rest of the work of that type—indeed, infinitely more so than the works of Géricault, David, Gérôme, and many others —exceedingly sterile and dry.

"Who remembers to-day," cries Ernest Chesneau in a superb comparison of Art before and after the return to realism, "the pseudo-classical painting composed coldly in the studio . . . invariably cut after the same pattern . . . a puzzle-game of patience in which every move was known before it was made ; melancholy productions of spirits turned aside by puerile idolatry ;—of arid brains adoring fetiches of their own creation ; of intelligences incapable of comprehending the sublime spectacle of truth?" This fine burst of enthusiasm is perhaps a trifle too severe in its condemnation, but without doubt the day when classical landscape appealed to the public taste had gone by even while Corot occasionally returned to burn some incense at the altar of its tradition, and we cannot see cause for anything but congratulation that as time passed he freed himself more and more from its shackles and gave himself completely to the expression of his own individuality.

As we have already said, Corot had some

distaste for vivid colouring in nature; he seems
to have disliked the display and self-assertion
expressed by it; yet he did not hesitate to
make use of it where he realised its value for
dramatic effect. In his study for the picture
of Hamlet the setting sun flames in the west
with a glow that would not have disgraced a
canvas of Turner, and in the "Destruction of
Sodom" the whole landscape is ablaze with
the lurid glare from the burning city. And it
was this picture which its author desired should
be the first one saved if destruction should at
any time threaten his studio. Dumesnil tells
us that at one time Corot was much occupied
with the work of Titian; he expresses his surprise at this fact, which was, however, stated
to him by the artist himself; and indeed there
is no outward sign of any influence of the
Venetian master upon Corot's work.

Corot was always keenly alive to the criticism of his brother artists, and the slightest
mention of his work in the early days aroused
his gratitude. When Alfred de Musset, therefore, in 1836, remarked that "Corot in his
'Roman Campagna' has found admirers,"
Corot was profoundly moved. He sought out
some lines of de Musset's, and, according to

SOLEIL COUCHANT

some critics, painted one of his best works on
the "Etoile du Soir."

"Pâle étoile du soir, messagère lointaine
  Dont le front sort brillant des voiles du couchant,
  De ton palais d'azur, au sein du firmament
    Que regardes-tu dans la plaine?"

It was always a matter of regret to Corot
that he had comparatively but little opportunity for decorative painting, a branch in
which he delighted.* Dumesnil rather wickedly
suggests that his predilection for this style of
painting may have been influenced by the fact
that it was quickly done. Indeed, Corot said,
"They go of themselves." The four great
panels representing four hours of the day
which he painted for the studio of his friend
Décamps were completed in one week, whilst
those ordered by Prince Demidoff took but
three months. Corot would have welcomed
similar orders from other architects, but these
were either unaware of the fact, or as the
artist himself said, "afraid of the holes which
he might make in their walls by the quantity
of air which he put into his pictures." Re-
ferring to the objections raised to Corot's
colour, Thomson speaks with irony of those

* A full description of all his frescoes will be found
in chapter ix.

persons who cannot value a man's colour unless he hits them in the eye with red, blue, and yellow, and calls attention to the delicacy and subtlety of open-air colours which he claims that Corot rendered with sincerity. R. A. M. Stevenson says of him: "Corot generally works on a composition made of broad, simply arranged, large masses. These he surrounds and overlays with a lovely lace-work of light branches and floating leaves."

Now that Corot has been recognised as a master, one whose paintings have a high market value—now that to possess a "Corot" is to possess an acknowledged treasure, it is amusing to be told that G. P. Chalmers, a Scotch Academician, as recently as the eighties, had the utmost difficulty in persuading the Royal Scotch Academy to hang a "Corot" at all. Would the private collectors in the north at the present day—and they are not a few—credit the fact that Corot was condemned and scorned in Scotland at the Exhibition of 1885-6?

CHAPTER VII

CRITICISM—CONTEMPORARY AND LATER

IT is always a matter of peculiar interest
in the face of the verdict pronounced by
another generation to re-read contemporary
criticism. From the mass that exists upon
Corot's work we have tried to select the most
vital, and present it to our readers to approve
or condemn according to their own individual
judgment.

Beyond the few words written by Jal and one
or two other critics in the very early days when
Corot was yet unknown (some of which we
have quoted elsewhere), little of any import-

ance appeared before the year 1838, when
Gustave Planche wrote as follows : " It would
be a pity if, in spite of everything, Corot allowed
himself to be discouraged by lack of popularity.
It were well if among the caravan loads of
painters who overrun France there were one
who despised vulgarity, and set himself to in-
troduce something new into landscape painting.
Whether they be counted successes or failures,
Corot's landscapes are a useful protest against
the dwarfed realism which menaces our school;
he, at any rate, concerns himself only with the
ideal."

T. Thoré, whose criticism on art of all
periods and schools was most trenchant, seems
to have had some difficulty in assigning Corot
any definite position. He began to write of
him as early as 1844, when he described the
pictures exhibited that year at the Salon with
much vigour ; but in 1847 he wrote of a small
landscape in a manner which proved him to be
entirely at one with the artist, to have penetrated for once to the very heart of the painter
and his work.

" ' Evening Effect.' A river ; in mid-stream
a boat, showing black ; groups of trees to right
and to left ; a distant lead-coloured sky in the
same twilight scheme of colour ; two notes

PAYSAGE NORMAND

only, a dark bistre and a pale silver, which unite in producing an effect of silence, dream-like and melancholy. Stand a moment before this little picture, with its first impression as of a confused sketch. You will feel the air, soft and scarcely stirring. You are enveloped in a diaphanous mist which floats over the river away into the distance until it is lost in the greenish tints of the sky on the horizon. You are aware of the almost imperceptible sounds of this quiet spot—the trembling of the leaves, the motion of a fish rising to the surface of the water. You feel all the peace of that evening when, resting after a day of toil at the water's edge, you watched for the night to show forth her first stars. If the aim of paint-ing be to communicate to others the artist's own feelings about nature, then Corot's land-scape fulfils every requirement of art."

And yet on another occasion this same critic writes of the same artist in the following words: "This cumbersome execution; this laboured drawing, although it achieves a cer-tain elegance; this plastered and lifeless colour-ing — all betray a great perseverance which has never attained to a mastery of the technique of his art. Corot is like a sensitive and eloquent man, whose language remains always a stranger to his thought. But in spite of this we have seen sketches of his, executed at one sitting, which, with their soft effects of light, are well able to hold their own by the side of more vigorous and striking paintings."

Edmond About, in 1855, in his *Voyage à travers l'Exposition*, introduces the name of Corot in the following manner: "Corot is a painter, unique, exceptional; he stands apart from all 'genres' and from all schools; he imitates nothing, *not even nature*, and is himself inimitable! No artist has more style, or knows better how to put his own ideas into a landscape. He transforms all that he touches; he appropriates all that he paints; he copies *never;* and even when painting directly from nature he invents. In passing through his imagination all objects reclothe themselves in vague and charming forms; colours soften and melt, all becomes young, fresh, harmonious."

In 1859 Paul Mantz summed up Corot in the following words: "Corot is a poet, a musician, a conjurer. He takes a brush, and with a few colours which are said to be always the same he evolves some confused forms, vague apparitions, monotonous foliage. It is little for the worshippers of technique, but for us it embodies Nature with her poetic melancholy, her intoxi-

cating freshness, all that is in her to awaken
love : the meadows and the woods. He is by
turns garrulous or religious, familiar or grand,
lyric or terrible."

Corot, who was aware of the oft-repeated
accusation of monotony against his work, himself said : "To see my landscapes truly one
must have patience to wait, at least, until the
mists begin to lift. One can penetrate but a
little way at a time, but once really there one
ought to be pleased."

It does not occasion us much surprise that
many persons spoke and thought of Corot's
work as monotonous. To how many of us is
not Nature herself monotonous and wearisome ?
To how many persons is not a beautiful view
in front of their windows tiresome, " always the
same "? It needs a poetic imagination to
recognise with Corot the varied beauties which
one scene will present in the course of a single
day under the constant changes of light and
shadow. How much more, then, when we take
into consideration the essential difference which
each season brings in its train?

Buisson once said that in the light of Corot's
teaching, nature appears to us more human,
more brotherly.

Ernest Chesneau in 1864 describes Corot's

I

landscapes as "beautiful dreams of awakening dawn, pictures of an imaginary world, the embryo of our world which is to follow. This fantastic country is like the prelude to a superior work. We realise that this unknown world is the first sketch for ours ; that later on the trees will grow green, the skies blue. . . . This new planet discovered by Corot is inhabited by pale forms bearing resemblance to mankind ; in the titles they are called nymphs, but I think they are, in truth, souls just born, making their first acquaintance with life."

Following, as we have continued to do, the sequence of years in which the criticisms were written, we now come to one which appeared in the *Art Journal* of 1867, and which read in the light of the estimation of later years bears an interest entirely its own. "Nature in France is often not a little peculiar, and French landscape painters willingly lend themselves to her eccentricities. Trees as straight and stripped as bare as maypoles adorn every Parisian Gallery. Flat, uneventful tracts of land are also the delight of the great nation. A German affects mountains, forests, lakes ; a French painter is content with a marsh, a moor, and a wind-stricken tree. It requires not a little skill to evoke a picture in the absence of a sub-

LE MARAIS

ject, and it is just this ready wit that the French possess. They generally, as in the works of Daubigny, Rousseau, and Corot, pitch their pictures in a low key. They often, by way of beginning, roll a black storm across the sky, bring a dark shadow over the foreground, and so at last the whole work gives solution to the problem how to make darkness visible. . . . Such painters as Corot scrub in a subject with dirt for colour; pictures of this sort, which abound, may be said to constitute 'The French school of dirty weather landscape.' That our neighbours, if outrageous, are yet original, no one will question."

Chaumelin, writing in the following year in *L'Art Contemporain*, says: "Corot has never been more inspired than in his 'Matin à Ville d'Avray.' A silver mist rises slowly over a marsh and envelops like a floating veil the shivering trees and tufts of grass, among which two white cows are grazing in the care of a little peasant girl. One can imagine nothing more exquisitely fresh; but one trembles lest the sun should come out, and in dispersing the vapours, carry away the whole thing, trees, cows, marsh, cowherd. The lightness of the colour, the breadth of touch, the sobriety of the detail, the extreme simplicity of effect, by all of which Corot obtains such surprising results, have been the means of seducing a number of artists who have perceived in all this only an authorisation to convenient negligence and incorrectness of drawing."

Up to this time—1868—it does not appear to have occurred to any of the critics that this peculiar quality of work introduced by Corot may have been the result, not of indifference to drawing, but of a most consummate art following upon untiring study; and an article in the *Portfolio* in 1870, touching upon this view, brings it forward with some caution, and more as a suggestion of a possibility than as a statement of fact.

"We may rely upon it that, after his fifty years with nature, that which to a very simple-minded critic appears ignorance in his work is not ignorance, whatever else it may be. In his present practice Corot cannot be said to draw anything whatever in the usual sense of the word drawing. There is a stage in Art *beyond* study, when after learning what has to be learnt, we look once more at nature with the wondering gaze of a child, and receive impressions without conscious analysis of their causes. To paint in this spirit requires either unusual courage or unusual simplicity of character, because criticism is sure to fall foul of any genuine poetical work and abuse it, and accuse the poet of ignorance or affectation."

In the same connection Buisson speaks of the "strength of his technique," "his inexplicable manner which was gained by forty years of struggle, or perhaps we ought rather to say alliance with nature." "Outside his poetic vision," Buisson continues, "Corot had little beyond one idea, hence the refusal of prosaic spirits to recognise his worth, since to them it appeared as though he only painted one landscape over and over again."

"Whether," wrote Buisson in the *Gazette des Beaux Arts*, "he stands at sunrise outside a village in Auvergne, enveloped in morning mists ; whether he stands before the Coliseum at evening, while the light before fading concentrates itself in the depths of the sky ; or whether he sketches a Franciscan monk meditating in the bright sunshine—he approaches all in the same unbiassed spirit, without preconceived system, letting himself be possessed and penetrated by the impression. That, indeed, is the secret of greatness. The master who produces a creation of strength and individuality does so by being impersonal in the face of nature." "It is in his great imagination that Corot's chief merit lies; it is through this that he has become the familiar of the demi-gods of painting. But shall we for all this any the more close our eyes to his weak points? Had he been possessed of the precision of a man of science there would have remained nothing for the landscape painter of the future!"

A. H. Bicknell in *Old and New* says: "Unless we study the most subtle phases of nature we must fail to see any merit in Corot's work. This is not surprising if we consider that he almost ignores drawing as it is technically understood. He deals frequently with the monotonous and dull in nature, with hardly a line or single mass worthy of a fine composi-tion; in truth, not unfrequently without a single object that is not stale and characterless." He goes on later to a description of a particular picture. "Before us hangs an exquisite Corot. We know full well that a ball of cotton stuck on a stick is not a tree, nor a patch of brown a cow—yet the picture is inexpressibly charm-ing, for Corot's greatness lies in the truthfulness of his values." "There is something singularly lowly and humble in Corot's artistic aspirations. What the world regards as the meanest forms and scenes of nature are fondly cherished by

LANDSCAPE

him ; but as though he were half conscious of
their insignificance to the world he indicates
but lightly their forms that he may the better
display their tender shades and tints. Majestic
trees are nothing to Corot the painter ; any
brushwood lifting its branches above the horizon
furnishes all he seeks. . . . Much as we admire
his work, we should not in strictness pronounce
him a great artist. True greatness compre-
hends more than can justly be claimed for him.
Corot seems to us a fragment of a great artist
—a noble and precious fragment, indeed, yet
wanting the breadth and intensity of thought
which distinguish the truly great painter. . . .
There is in Corot's work a monotony. He
rarely gives us a surprise. Yet there is an
indescribable pensiveness in all that he does,
which, if it does not appeal to our imagination,
touches our tenderest sympathies. . . . There
is no evidence in his work from the beginning
of there being anything beyond for which he
is striving. . . . There is a complacency per-
vading all his productions which . . . points
unerringly to the narrow limits of his capacity
as an artist, and shows the want of that uni-
versality of love and mastery of nature which
is the sure index of the broad and compre-
hensive mind of a great artist."

We have quoted at great length from the above article, not because we are in sympathy with its sentiments, but rather because they differ in tone from almost all other existing criticism. We would ask our readers to compare them with the opinions of Frederick Wedmore and R. A. M. Stevenson. The former says : " As a landscape painter Corot stood alone. . . . Nothing could well be further from the decisive and emphatic genius of Constable than this genius of Corot, which lost and found itself in the subtlest intricacies of aërial effect. Moonlight, a placid sunset ; the freshness of the morning—mists quivering over the river, and the budding of trees in spring—these things he painted with a sentiment no living artist has been near to rivalling."

R. A. M. Stevenson, speaking of his basis of inspiration and his formation of a special style, points out the markedly stronger individuality of Corot's developed final manner to that of the slightly earlier painters, who had freed themselves from the bonds of classical tradition. He remarks that Crome and Constable bear more resemblance to their models, Hobbema and Rubens, than they do to Corot, although the latter was a contemporary and largely influenced by the same environment as they, whereas Hobbema and Rubens were of the sixteenth and seventeenth centuries. Stevenson entirely disclaims for Corot any indifference to technique, and considers that he paid the utmost attention to the amount of paint he put on his canvas, as well as to the disposition of every detail of his picture. "Style, after all," says Stevenson, "is no more than the decorative character and quality of paint pressed into the service of expression; no more, in fact, than keys of colour, proportion of masses and details, relative scales of definition, methods of handling, etc., used in a manner appropriate to the truths the painter wishes to convey. . . . Thus, for instance, the facts cannot be big ones and the treatment small and mean. In his later work Corot attained a perfect harmony of matter and manner; his style was founded solely on nature, invented to render his impressions. The featheriness, a natural property of real trees, Corot has expressed more eloquently than any man. . . . He was, in spite of his vaporousness, admirably conscientious in his modelling of large masses and of suggesting the smallest detail only so far as he could do it without sacrifice of what is greater."

From the above criticism, that of Comyns Carr in the *Contemporary* differs essentially.

"With all his originality, Corot was not a strong revolutionist in art. His perception, though true and delicate, was not sufficiently profound to penetrate to the heart of his subject." Comyns Carr speaks of Corot as a "lyric" painter, and remarks that in his work everything is subjugated by the sky, explaining that even the water in his pictures only serves to reflect the skies, and that the grass is pale grey and not green beneath the reflection of white clouds.

Madame van Rensselaer has summed up Corot's aims in these words: "What he wanted to repeat were not Nature's statistics, but their sum total; not her minutiæ, but the result she had wrought with them; not the elements with which she had built up a landscape, but the landscape itself."

"To insist upon special *motifs* and to sacrifice the rest" was, according to Jean Rousseau, Corot's chief characteristic. "Whether," writes Albert Wolff, "it be the old bridge of Mantes seen through the branches of the big trees, which cast their reflection in the translucent waters, or the Garda Lake extended as far as eye can see in the morning light, the breeze stirring the leaves along its borders, it is the country itself which this enchanter knows how to place upon his canvas, the country in all its moods—the roseate dews of the morning, the rising moisture of the approaching night; of the serenity of nature, Corot is the interpreter *par excellence*."

In all the variety of opinion collected here under the guise of criticism we are struck by the absence of any real criticism from Corot's compatriots. Most of the French writers have treated Corot as a poet and a dreamer, and in their estimate of his work have either understood too little of its quality to be able to examine its excellences, or have feared to take from his renown as a poet-painter by showing what an immensity of study and careful execution went to the completion of his slightest sketch. Corot's aim was to ally style with a love of nature, and although he spent his life in the struggle to prove to others the truths which he recognised, he was in the end victorious. Although some critics are yet to be found who object to his methods of painting, none now deny the nobility of his aim, or that he lent poetry and sentiment to that which had become but conventional composition, lacking alike both life and truth. That Corot was the creator of a new art we do not for one moment pretend. The movement was in the air. It

had been started by Crome and followed by
Constable, taken up by Huet, Cabat, Rousseau, and others before Corot had in any
degree emancipated himself from the teachings
of his early masters; but although he but
carried on an art which his contemporaries
had revived from a former generation, he, by
the help of his superb genius, imbued it with a
new spirit, and was able to force upon the unwilling critics and public of his day recognition
of the eternal beauty of this re-embodied truth.

But perhaps even more than on the subject
of Corot's greatness as an artist did opinions
differ on the matter of his pastorals with their
nymphs and fauns. Indeed, the question of
figures in rural landscape had become a burning
one, and the artists of the day intentionally
emphasised their views either by consistently
putting in or by steadily leaving out the human
form. Cabat used to say, "Let us be true;
Nature will take care to be beautiful; she
needs neither heroes nor naiades."

Jean Rousseau, in describing pictorial art at
the time of Corot's birth, says that like the
literature of the period, it had to be "grandiose
or nothing. There were no rivers, only tor-
rents; no houses, only Greek temples; no
peasants, only nymphs and shepherds; no

DANSE ANTIQUE

familiar trees—nothing but cedars and palms."
This "pseudo-classical" school was careful to
place groups of figures in their landscapes to
accentuate the note—a concession to tradition
which was largely responsible for the entire
absence of figures in the early works of the
"naturalist" school. Chesneau accuses the
earlier painters of being governed by a terror
of solitude, or of being at the best entirely unconscious—reprehensibly unconscious, he calls
it—of its ennobling effect upon the soul. "The
figure," he says, "that the landscape painter
of to-day omits is replaced by the spectator,
who, living and breathing in the landscape,
communicates to the scene the human interest
most desired by himself."

With the old school the figure was para-
mount. They created or adapted a landscape
only to form a background to the heroic figures
they desired to paint. The new school wor-
shipped nature as exemplified outside the
human form. They deliberately selected a site
from which they could exclude all human
interest. Thoré, in writing of Titian and
Correggio, remarks: "It was not everyday
Italy that they painted there—it was an imaginary and apocryphal Greece; while the noble
Poussin, following in their footsteps, invented

Egyptian, Indian, Athenian landscapes at Rome." Describing further the style of work executed by painters of the classical school, Thoré proceeds to catalogue that of a popular painter of Van Dyck's time. He gives 1,460 paintings, of which about 1,400 were of the heroic type, or were portraits of princes or heroes. "But man as man," says Thoré, "he was not there at all; he had yet to be invented!"

Corot, as it were, held the balance between these two extremes. Trained by his early masters to a great respect for the classical tradition, drawn by inclination to the rural, he was able in a large measure to profit by both views. The beauty of a landscape was by no means impaired in his eyes by the figure of a peasant in its midst; indeed, being of a kindly nature with a distinct desire for companionship, he preferred the introduction of the figures, without which he often said, "no place appeared habitable." "His figures, whether that of a fisherman at the side of a pool, or of a peasant strolling down an avenue," says Albert Wolff, "are never thrown haphazard into the picture; they serve to mark the union of the country with that which lives in her." With this opinion Rousseau is in accord. "Corot's

figures," he says, "enhance his landscape; the
latter is not formed from scraps borrowed from
many sources after the figures are once there,
but all lives together — figures, landscape,
everything!" It is evident that to Corot himself his figures were real. "Do you see that
shepherdess?" he asked a friend, indicating a
figure in his picture leaning against a tree.
"She is turning quickly, because she hears
a *mulot* stirring in the grass."

Hardly has he sketched the contours of a
forest when nymphs and cupids, radiant children of the poetic fancy, escape from every
corner, and come to people the beautiful shades
of his creation.

"There are moments when the incomparable
grandeur of the sites he selects forces the artist's
dreams towards the mystic, and he translates
the whispering of the leaves by the figures of
nymphs and fauns, much as the poet thinks to
distinguish spirit voices in the murmurs of the
wind." Thus charmingly do Ed. About and
A. Wolff describe a scene of which René-
Ménard complains in the following terms:
"Poussin was at least logical, and placed his
figures in appropriate surroundings; but these
fresh vapours of Corot's woods, how do they fit
with the half-nude nymphs who only go about

so lightly clad because they never catch cold? These damp and muddy places may be suitable for cattle, but the naiades are out of place at the edge of a pool." To plant a mythological scene in a wood in France appears to Ménard a contradiction with which he is not in sympathy, but indeed it is a fact that Corot's imagination is not of the order that delights altogether in nymphs and dryads. Corot, who can invest the commonest landscape with romance, has not the true pastoral feeling. He presents us with a woodland scene such as the most prosaic person sees as he passes through the woods in the season when the wild-flowers are blossoming in the undergrowth. The addition to this scene of a group of pastoral figures—be they as entrancing and graceful as Corot may succeed in making them—yet fails to convert the painting into a pastoral. Again and again, in the atmosphere with which he has surrounded them, among their grassy glades fading into a fairy-like blue distance, does Watteau's most pronounced assemblage of courtiers and fine ladies form a far more complete and satisfying pastoral than anything which left the hands of Corot. Indeed, it is only in what we may term his domestic type of landscape that

Corot's instinct in placing figures is unerring. His peasants in the fields and paths add a touch of completeness of which we should feel the absence the instant they were withdrawn. Often in his forest scenes, with their luxuriance of greenery, the wild freedom in which the trees have expanded, flinging their arms wide in the ecstasy of existence, we should prefer to feel that no human foot had trod, and yet these very scenes are often marred by the presence of a fisherman. We cannot but feel that it is only from a desire to conciliate the classical tradition that Corot so constantly placed a punt and an occupant on a weed-grown lake to indulge in an aimless peregrination in a spot where the presence of a boat has not the slightest *raison d'être*. Yet not the less true is Jean Rousseau's exclamation on this same question of mythology: " How differently from his professors did Corot understand this ! How he rejuvenated it ! Does there exist another example of treatment so fresh of themes so superannuated ? "

K

CHAPTER VIII

METHODS OF PAINTING

The secret of Corot's genius—Actual methods described
by Philippe Burty—Tone numbers—Several distinct
methods—Form more important than detail—George
Moore and Corot—Recognition of values—Makes his own
laws and abides by them—All great genius prolific—
Historic landscape—Poussin—Claude Lorrain—The
"*style champêtre*"—Crome—Constable—Bonington—
Corot not directly influenced by Constable—Nature's
mobility—Corot essentially a dreamer—No conscious
methods—No mannerisms.

"COROT, as one may say, painted with
wings on his shoulders." This was the
verdict of one of his contemporaries, Jules
Dupré, himself an artist of strong individuality,
who rose to fame in a much shorter time than
the friend he extolled.

"Critics are at a loss," says Edmond About,
"to discover the secret of his genius. One
sees well that his pictures are flooded with
light, yet how does he contrive to paint air?
His water is of an intoxicating limpidity; but
live ten years in his studio and one would not

THE WOOD-GATHERER

learn to imitate it. His trees are without contour and without colour, but how can they be? He does not know himself. He says to himself, 'I will paint a sunset.' He takes his brushes and his palette, he sketches in trees and water and people, but he is not thinking of them, he is dreaming of his setting sun. The work finished and exhibited, you, too, notice neither the people, the water, nor the trees, you only exclaim, 'What a lovely sunset!'"

Corot's own answer to the above remarks may be found in the following words : " Is it possible for us to reproduce the sky, water, a tree ? No ; it is only possible to give the appearance of so doing. We must endeavour to give the impression of movement, though this be almost intangible. Suppose I paint a wheel, the spokes of which I cannot distinguish ; I must show that they are turning. With the sky it is different, that is still, deep, or mobile—full of vibrations which arrest the eye. And the effect? Oh! that is not very easy to attain!"

Of his actual methods of painting we have little evidence. Philippe Burty, in his introductory note to the Catalogue of the Posthumous Sale, repeats a description given him by one of Corot's pupils. "He was in the habit of using canvases which were fastened on keyed stretchers not very tightly strained. He was careful to avoid any such covering as would, from the nature of its preparation, cause the painting to crack. The canvas was always of the best quality obtainable, sometimes lightly tinted." Corot laid in his ground-work with raw umber, black and white, heightened by raw and burnt sienna and good ochres, but never used any of the bitumen so much in vogue at that time. He sketched in his subject with white chalk, and with such precision that he rarely found occasion to alter it at all. He used an ordinary palette, which he set out with strong colours, but without much system or care, and rather large and very strong brushes.

A pupil explained that his method of work in the studio was purely by tonality, and he certainly appears to have laid the plans of his pictures on these lines. For the convenience of noting effects when on a journey, or at a time when it would have been impossible to paint, Corot devised a system of numbering from one to four. Thus the number one on a rough sketch denoted the deepest shadow, number four the highest light, and the two intermediate

numbers distinguished two important intermediate tones.   In this way he retained vivid
impressions of cloud effects on any scrap of
paper which came to hand ; and of which his
marvellous memory for lights and shades, forms
and tones, greatly increased the value.

According to R. A. M. Stevenson, Corot had
several distinct methods.   He tells us that the
artist commonly selected a fine canvas with a
good "tooth" on it and very little preparation.
Upon this he smudged in very thinly his main
masses of tone, modelling them loosely and
broadly.   Then he worked into the wet paint
darker and lighter spots of detail, and finally
the last exquisite touches of finish. Sometimes,
however, he laid in the whole canvas thickly
and heavily, and before finishing scraped it
down to a thin ghost of itself.   Sometimes he
laid on the paint thickly all through and painted
straight ahead, and in some of his work he
adopted two of these processes on one canvas.
" It took Corot years of study and a thousand
half-failures," Stevenson tells us, " to imagine
the technical devices that enabled him to give
true relief to his idea. The grain of the canvas,
the fluidity of the vehicle, the use of impasto,
the flick into wet paint, the retouched scrape,
the quick upward drag of the rigger, the

smudged texture—all these things had to be considered and practised before the finest Corots were produced." "The principles he established were chiefly that light must be preferred before local colour; the growth of a stem before the markings on its bark; that modelling must be held of greater importance than leaf drawing; that you must ever observe the general aspects that nature wears at various distances from your foreground."

Corot himself told A. Marx how in the early days of his painting from nature he walked miles over one picture, just going backwards a few paces from his easel to see the effect of each touch and advancing again to alter it. George Moore recounts an occasion upon which he came upon Corot painting in the Forest of Fontainebleau. He approached the master and stood awhile looking on at his work. Corot turned and asked him how it pleased him. Moore expressed his admiration, but asked the artist from what point in the landscape this picture was taken, as he could not see at all where it came from. Corot pointed to a distance of some couple of hundred yards which was the foreground of his sketch.

Moore attributes all the beauty of Corot's work to his complete recognition of values.

He avers that the relations of the half-tint to the highest light need, in painting, examination on two points ; that of the relative amount of colouring matter as well as the proportion of light and shade. "No colour can be said to be in itself either false or true, ugly or beautiful," he remarks ; but only in its relation to its surroundings is it to be appraised, and it is in his complete recognition and comprehension of these matters that Corot's genius triumphs. All these theories are interesting enough and probably correct up to a certain point, but as there is actually no guarantee that any one of them is based upon Corot's own words, we may conclude that they are the result of the observation of various individuals, each of whom has used his opportunity to study Corot's work and form his own conclusions as to the method employed for its completion. Unfortunately none of us can now enjoy the privilege which fell to the lot of some of these critics, that of seeing the master at work, but we would recommend any student of landscape painting to examine the finished work in the light of these descriptions, study them as his predecessors have done, and then, if he be able, evolve a theory of Corot's brushwork for his own use. We recollect a significant remark

of one of the most famous art critics of
Corot's day. "It is scarcely possible," he
said, standing in front of a certain landscape,
"to decide whether Corot paints with his
hands or with his feet!"

From the above criticisms it would seem then
that the conclusion to be drawn is that Corot had
not—as so many painters have—any special line
of action; he saw the end and he made direct for
it, regardless of, or indifferent to, the route; he
knew well that he would attain his goal, for
he was well prepared to meet any and every
difficulty that the way might present. Not only
did he possess inspiration—that alone could
have been submerged—but he possessed also
mastery of means. His art had risen above
the need for regular methods; he had studied
and worked until his fingers were able to
respond mechanically to the dictum of his
brain, and sooner or later he knew that the
canvas would live with the life of that nature
which it represented.

Corot was always eager to record any impression which had particularly struck him,
and in order to place the impression in the
right surroundings, he was in the habit of
adapting one of his existing sketches to the
new idea. Dumesnil tells us how he would

UNE MATINÉE

hasten to his studio with his head full of some
design. Then he would place a row of canvases side by side on the floor, the whole
length of the studio, and select from amongst
them the one in whose tones he saw *son affaire*.
Without waiting to scrape or in any way pre-
pare the canvas, he would seize a paint-brush
and with almost feverish eagerness proceed to
execute his object, fearing by delay to lose the
idea. "It would give my conception time to
evaporate ; I might forget it, and that would
never do," he would exclaim. "It is, above
all, the idea that we must have, so we will put
it down at once." "But in spite of this apparent haste," says Dumesnil, "Corot never
made an uncalculated stroke ; he had studied
greatly, had made laws of his own, and he
never either forgot or broke them."

Clarétie complains that people not only re-
proach Corot with his individuality, but also
with his fecundity. "The idle and the weak
have always disliked the industrious," he remarks, "whereas many critics maintain that
all great genius is prolific."

The artists whose careers are of the greatest
interest are always those who, like Corot, lived
at the end of one period and the beginning of
the next ; who, walking at first in the beaten

track, soon discover that they are on the road which leads to destruction, while before them lie concealed glories to which they need but to force a way to find and possess them.

In a treatise on landscape painting, much quoted at the beginning of the nineteenth century, J. B. Deperthes described Historic Landscape as the art of gathering together in one composition all that nature can produce of nobility and beauty; of introducing such figures and personages as create by their action an ideal, or serve to illustrate some historic deed calculated to impress the spectator with the highest sentiments. "To achieve this, one must be possessed of a lively imagination, a pure taste, and the habit of meditation." In this treatise, the handbook of the student of landscape of the day, Deperthes, while insisting upon the soundest tuition, recommends the student to a study of Nature in all her moods.

Impressions thus gained are to be recorded, not at the moment, but on the return to the studio, there enriched by the imagination, and formed into a picture in accordance with the traditions handed down by Poussin and Claude Lorrain. These two masters, it is said, brought to their studios stones, shells, and moss, in order, by a faithful reproduction of

these minutiæ, to give a semblance of reality
to their compositions. For the so-called "*style
champêtre*" Deperthes had nothing but contempt. "It is that," he said, "which retraces
with exactitude the faithful picture of a scene
in all its details, and fixes on the canvas, line
for line, a landscape with the portion of sky
which dominates it and the actual light which
illumines it at the precise moment when the
artist is occupied with its reproduction."
Criticism of a somewhat similar kind might
well be offered to some of the landscape
painters of to-day, in the hope of enabling
them to see how lifeless a picture of nature
is the result of such methods. Beneath the
loving study and faithful reproduction of nature
to be found, it is true, in Corot's work, real
light illumines, the sky glows, the landscape
quivers with the life that quickens it, and
Nature reveals herself in fresh beauty to him
who goes direct to her for inspiration.

But the teachers of that day ignored this
truth, and Valenciennes considered nature-
sketching in the open-air to be a useless waste
of time.

But the new school of landscape-painting
grew apace. "Poussin and his school," says
Dumesnil, "had been imitated and copied until

pictures called landscapes, badly conceived and worse executed, resembled nature about as much as do the toy trees and woods which are given to children as playthings." Already in England the elder Crome had begun to return to the natural style in vogue in the Dutch and Flemish pictures of a bygone day. Constable and Bonington quickly recognised his wisdom, and followed him. Already Bonington and Fielding had begun to show in their water-colours the luminous qualities of their melancholy skies. They had begun to show that the north possessed beauties equal to, if differing in quality from, those of the south, and that to become a landscape painter of merit it was not so requisite to go to Italy for inspiration as it was to discover the beauties lying around one, and then to learn how to place those beauties on canvas without the aid of "composition."

Although the first picture which Corot sent to the Salon (1827) chanced to be hung between a Constable and a Bonington, he was by no means the French pioneer of the movement. Dupré, Huet, Daubigny, Cabat, were all alive to its truth, and working along the same lines when Corot decided that this was the right path. That he soon distanced these friends

and contemporaries is true, but that is due
rather to his greater genius than to his holding
stronger convictions.   There is no evidence
that Corot was consciously influenced at any
time by Constable's work; so generous a
nature as his would have certainly recorded
any debt of gratitude owed to any teacher, and
there is little doubt that had Constable never
existed, Corot would yet have entered the
promised land, and found his way direct to
fame, led by the hand of Mother Nature herself.   To love is to comprehend, and Corot was
from childhood a nature lover.   What wonder,
then, that he was aware of beauties unknown
to the ordinary mortal, to whom, however, he,
by means of his paintings, opened a new
world.   Gustave Colin said that "Corot painted
less Nature as she is than the love he bears
her," but is not Rousseau's definition the truer,
that "he does better than merely copy and
reproduce; he suppresses useless detail, thus
bringing to light nature's true aspect."   Corot
himself used to lay great stress upon the
mobility of nature, and it is this peculiar
quality seen in his work which some have
called indecision, but it is its very existence
which leads us to realise the constant changes
in nature, the movement of life, that makes his

representations so vibrant, that lends them
their charm.   R. A. M. Stevenson maintains
that he has taught us that "truths will assume
on our canvases just the proportion of importance which we have accorded them in our
observation of nature.   If we are as earnest
in observation of the trivial as of the essential,
we shall infallibly overstate the small and let
the large go unexpressed."   Delacroix, in ex-
ceeding contempt of the teaching of the day,
exclaims: "This beauty in which they see
nothing but the harmony and proportion between two lines I see an exquisite landscape;
not an idea of a line comes to me.   To them
all is chaos which cannot be defined by the
compass."

Yet if we compare Corot with a later master,
say with Bastien Lepage in "Les Foins," we
realise how difficult a matter it is to free
oneself entirely from old tradition.   Corot is
nearer in spirit to the old classicist aiming at
depicting only the noble and heroic than he is
to the naked exposure of brutal truths undertaken by Lepage.   Corot is essentially a
dreamer.   He did not see the hopelessness of
that phase of life—should we rather say existence?—which Lepage wrote so clearly upon

the faces of his labourers.   When, as in some
of his pictures, a pig strays across one of
Corot's canvases, we feel that it has lost its
way, and is there only by accident ; the more
poetic forms are those we look to see, and when
we find sheep or cows grazing in his meadows,
we realise that that is as it should be and all
is in harmony.   Coming as he did at the
moment when landscape painters had begun to
revolt against composition as a chief factor
in their branch of art, Corot imbibed both influences — that of the harmonious and classic
past with the new movement towards a faithful
rendering of Nature as she is; he arrived at
the *juste milieu*, which combined the best of
both periods, and which placed him in the
front rank of landscape painters.

Corot had no conscious methods.   He felt
as an idealist, he painted as a realist, and the
former quality saved him from an all too dreary
view of the nature he studied in all its aspects ;
and his true presentment of the landscape before him as his eyes saw it gave the strength
and convincing quality which his predecessors
had lacked.   Corot's art speaks alike to all.

He has no mannerisms.   De Langenevois
said of him very justly that his chief character-

istic is an absence of applied method. It is
true.   Corot viewed nature with the eye of
romance, and adopted the simplest means of
conveying his meaning to the canvas.   That a
great art lies concealed under this simplicity is
a fact that none will question.   Jean Rousseau
said that "to capture nature alive on the
wing" was Corot's mission; and to fulfil this
mission, of which he was well aware, necessitated constant observation and ceaseless study:
and his end he achieved.   His paintings are
always fresh with the freshness of eternal
youth, the youth of Art that can never grow
old because of the spring of Life which it is
always generating.

Corot was eminently a lover of nature.   No
spot but is beautiful in his sight; the most
commonplace landscape springs into beauty
under the loving touch of the master hand.
Just as a scene otherwise gloomy and dull is
transformed by the sunlight into a thing of
beauty, so a group of sordid cottages, a
labourer tramping a dusty road, a stagnant
pond in a tangle of undergrowth, are transformed by this poet-painter's hand into an
Arcadian world of rest and peace.   Every
cottage becomes a haven, every labourer sees

LA ROUTE DE SÈVRES

the welcome awaiting him in the home to which he is wending his way; every pool is the trysting-place of the nymphs and shepherds whose figures flit so frequently through the dusky glades of those deep woods which Corot loved to paint.

CHAPTER IX

FRESCOES AND DECORATIVE WORK

Corot's special gifts for the work—What frescoes should be
—Many of his wall-paintings not true frescoes—Four
frescoes in Ville d'Avray Church—Their reproduction—
Prince Paul Demidoff's "Hotel"—Panels for Décamps
—Frescoes purchased by Sir Frederic Leighton—Corot
and Fleury— M. Giraud's screen—Madame Corot's
birthday—The paintings in the summer-house—Panels
at Daubigny's house — M. Robert's bath-room—M.
Robaut's criticisms—Minor decorative work—Design for
tapestry-panel—M. Rodrigues' palette.

COROT once expressed regret that he so
rarely received a commission for decorative work in fresco. He believed that he
possessed a special gift for work of this kind,
and it must be allowed that there was justifica-
tion for his belief. He was certainly incapable
of falling into the error, not an uncommon one,
as he points out, in decorative paintings, of
representing foliage which looks "as though it
had been cut out of metal; the only light
shining upon it, that which had penetrated in
blotches through the windows of the studio

where the design was originally conceived and created." Frescoes, to bear all the charm of which they are capable, must be fresh in treatment and quickly executed. Corot's peculiarly light touch lends itself admirably to this sort of work ; his frescoes "went of themselves," as he told a friend on one occasion.

M. Robaut held that the initial difference between easel and decorative work lies in the fact that a picture in a frame is movable, and that therefore its position can be changed at any time, whilst a decorative painting is fixed. He claims for Corot all the requisites for a successful decorative painter. A decorative painting requires simplicity of treatment, whilst at the same time it should represent nature in a most alluring aspect, and its execution exacts much experience, much study, and a retentive memory. These qualities Corot possessed to the full.

We cannot but feel regret that so little of Corot's decorative work was actually "fresco," since much of that which was simply painted in oil directly upon the walls to be decorated has either already entirely disappeared or is fast peeling off, notably the four panels painted in the church of Ville d'Avray, which are rapidly disappearing. We have

M. Robaut to thank for the fact that four replicas of these fine works were made at a later date by Corot. Doubtless M. Robaut foresaw the fate that would inevitably overtake the originals, but he tells us that the plea he used to urge their reproduction was that the size and shape of the church walls had not been sufficiently taken into consideration when the paintings were made, with the result that many of their beauties were entirely hidden from the spectator, whilst some parts had even the appearance of being out of drawing and proportion.

The four paintings, which are all in the transept, are " Adam and Eve chased from Paradise," " Magdalen at Prayer," " Baptism of Christ by St. John," and " Christ in the Garden of Olives." M. Robaut gives the following description of these frescoes :—

" Adam and Eve chased from Paradise." The angel with the flaming sword appears from a thicket, and with a majestic gesture commands the departure of the culprits.

" The Baptism of Christ." Nothing can exceed the grace of the general outline of this landscape, and the transparency of the water of the lake, its surface lightly ruffled by a passing boat, conveying some passengers.

This composition differs entirely from the one on the same subject in the church of St. Nicholas du Chardonnet in Paris, although the central figures in each bear some slight resemblance one to another; those in the Ville d'Avray are less academic and proportionately more beautiful.

"Christ in the Garden of Olives." The night effect, strongly accentuated, brings into relief the halo around the head of Christ; this at the first glance renders the figure somewhat heavy, yet makes it only the more human in its abandonment. The attitude, as well as the colouring, of the angel, who is presenting a chalice, conveys an infinite tenderness in an atmosphere enveloped in mystery.

The picture of the "Magdalen" is dismissed with a comment upon the beautiful movement, noble expression, and fine contour of the landscape.

From a story which we have told elsewhere we learn that although Corot deprecated the small amount of work put into a certain picture painted for a patron, he was rather disposed to consider amongst his best works those which came, as it were, with the greater spontaneity. It is certain that some of his frescoes were painted in an almost incredibly short time, and it is possible that this fact may have enhanced the value in the artist's own estimation.

In the year 1865 Prince Paul Demidoff entrusted the completion of an "hotel" for his own habitation in Paris to the clever architect, Alfred Feydeau. This gentleman decided to have some of the walls frescoed. He therefore commissioned Corot, Millet, Rousseau, and Fromentin to make designs, placing two walls at the disposition of Corot, from whom, too, he appears to have requested a more immediate execution of the order than he did from the other artists employed. Corot had at that time no studio which he considered suitable for the execution of so large an undertaking. He installed himself, therefore, in that of his friend Comaires, at Fontainebleau.

The subjects of the panels are "Morning" and "Evening," and three months were occupied in their completion. Although this appears to be an almost impossible feat as to time, it was slow work compared with that accomplished for Décamps, in whose studio Corot painted four panels representing four different hours of a day. These, it is said, were begun and finished in one week. The extra time expended upon the frescoes for Prince Paul may have been partially occupied in alterations of

NYMPHS AND FAUN

the original design, for there exist at least three sketches and a photograph of one of the panels, each containing some initial difference from the one actually delivered to Prince Paul. M. Georges Petit is the possessor of a canvas bearing the date 1868, which is indeed a replica of the same work, but contains slight changes in the attitude of the original figures and the addition of the figure of a cupid.

The works which the other artists furnished for Prince Paul Demidoff were a "Sunset" and a "Spring Day," by Rousseau; two forest scenes by Dupré; and a "Diana at the Bath" and "Scene with Centaurs" by Fromentin.

The four decorative panels alluded to above as painted for Décamps are semi-classical landscapes. These are notable for the light and graceful treatment so particularly appropriate to this branch of art. Of the four landscapes, two contain water and two are without; but they are all marked by a noble distinction of effect.

At the death of Décamps in 1860 the four frescoes were purchased by Sir Frederic Leighton,* who was a great admirer of the French master. Corot exercised this favourite mode of painting in favour of many of his

* At his death they passed into the possession of Lord Wantage.

friends. At Leon Fleury's house at Magny-les-Harneaux he painted four scenes on four walls of one room.

It was with this friend, one of his earliest and most intimate, that in the student days Corot worked constantly, and he considered their styles to resemble each other so nearly as to make it almost impossible to distinguish one from the other. On the back of a certain canvas Corot wrote: "We do not know, Fleury and I, which of us executed this study." But Fleury held another estimate of their respective values in art, and at a later date he wrote: "We marched together as far as life and work were concerned, but you are the only one who really rose, for the rest of us lacked the wherewithal."

There is an amusing story told of a screen which was to be presented by Armaud Leleux to his father-in-law, M. Giraud. It appears that M. Giraud possessed a very large drawing-room, which was uncomfortably pervaded by draughts. In order to protect his father-in-law Leleux ordered a carpenter to make a large six-fold screen, stretched with canvas for painting. Upon the arrival of the screen, seized with alarm apparently at the amount of labour the covering of so much canvas would entail,

Leleux appealed to Daubigny, who was a frequent visitor at the house, to come to his assistance in the matter.

At this period of their lives Corot, Leleux, and Daubigny had an arrangement to meet each alternate summer in Switzerland for a sketching tour.

The summer following the advent of the newly-made screen was the one in which the friends were to meet as usual. The weather was execrable, but fortune favoured Leleux. There were weeks of rain, when it was an impossibility to sketch out-of-doors. The friends smoked, played cards, and bored themselves and each other. Suddenly Corot was seized with an inspiration on the subject of the screen. He would paint the centre panel himself. The happy idea was no sooner conceived than it was put into execution; the screen was sent for, the work went on apace, and while Corot devoted himself to the middle of the canvas, Daubigny and Leleux turned their attention to the border, with the result that it was in all respects worthy of that which it enclosed. The screen represents a wide stretch of landscape; the sun setting gently behind a distant sweep of blue hills. In the middle distance rises a walled and fortified town; the foreground is occupied by a rocky waste, partially covered by low bushes; and a slope on the right is crowned with a fine group of trees. The landscape is surrounded by a trellis overgrown with vines in bloom, round and through the interstices of which some birds are flitting. The centre bears on a stone the date and signature "Corot, 1853"; on the sides in smaller letters are the names of Daubigny and Armaud Leleux.

Let us hope that the three artists were rewarded for their industry by some fine weather, indeed, we do not see how the sun could possibly have continued to sulk and hide itself in face of the subtle flattery and cajolery conveyed in the subjects of the paintings on the screen.

In 1849 Corot decided to surprise his mother on her birthday by painting the walls of a summer-house in the garden of their villa at Ville d'Avray. He selected only local views, and Robaut, who describes them as *bourgeois*, says they lack the distinction common to the artist's work. The most interesting of the six is undoubtedly one in which he reproduced the summer-house itself and introduced his own portrait and portraits of his family.

In the picture his father is standing quite in

the foreground, his brother-in-law approaching to meet him, his mother and sister are leaning upon the railing of a little bridge in the background, and the artist himself is on his way to the house with a portfolio. When, at Corot's death, the property of Ville d'Avray was sold, the purchaser had these frescoes removed with the utmost care.

At Daubigny's house Corot also painted several panels. Daumier, who had undertaken the first ones, had a passion for the story of Don Quixote, and he selected for the subject of his picture a scene from the life of his favourite hero, with his horse. Seeing this, Corot continued with another illustration, introducing in addition to the figures of Don Quixote and Rosinante that of Sancho Panza as well.

Corot used to spend many holidays at the house of an old family friend, a Mme. Osmond, who resided in the neighbourhood of Mantes, at the little village of Rosny. This village figured in many of Corot's paintings, and in one at least he reproduced its chief object of interest, the ruins of a small château, which had been the birthplace of the great Sully.

One of Mme. Osmond's neighbours, a certain M. Robert, was a nephew of hers. With this gentleman Corot soon stood in the close

bonds of friendship. Calling at M. Robert's
house one day when the gentleman happened
to be absent from home, Corot found the
house in the possession of painters and de-
corators who were just about to deal with the
bath-room. Corot, who, as a matter of fact,
was idling, had actually gone out without his
painting gear. But his artistic instincts were
always to the fore. Whether the smell of the
paint inspired him, or the sight of the newly-
cleaned flat surfaces overcame him, we do not
know; but he seized upon the colours, paint-
pots, and brushes that were there, turned out
his "colleagues," as he called them, and began
operations with his own hand. The bath-room
was small and of very irregular shape. These
drawbacks did not in the least affect Corot.
He measured the surfaces and set to work.
Robert had a predilection for Italian scenery;
of such should be the pictures which were to
spring to life on the bath-room walls. A view
called by courtesy the Gulf of Genoa occupied
the largest space. This view might, in fact,
have borne any other title with equal veracity.
It is a composed landscape; trees and rocks
fill the foreground, disclosing in the middle
distance between their trunks a castle on some

heights, and a glimpse of blue sea showing just below the horizon.

The next panel bears the title "Gorge in the Tyrol," and represents a cataract falling between the precipitous sides of a mountain gorge crowned with foliage. In the left-hand corner of the picture is a little white rabbit, and considerable doubt has been cast upon the authenticity of the small intruder. Some persons, believing the little figure to have been added by another hand than Corot's, have expressed great indignation at this supposed desecration, regarding it as a serious lack of adequate appreciation of the master's creations; but there is a strong probability that the rabbit was really put there by Corot himself, for a twin brother rabbit enjoys life in a very beautiful sketch, also painted at Rosny, and undoubtedly entirely the work of the master himself. A large square panel in the bath-room is filled by a magnificent scene on the "Lake of Némi." Above the window is a delightful view of the Grand Canal, Venice, glowing in all the freshness and enchantment of the magic city itself. The left-hand side of the window is decorated with another classical landscape, displaying the title "Naples," but bearing no resemblance to any particular spot near Naples or elsewhere ; and the right-hand side, a larger space, shows a delicious glimpse of the cupola of St. Peter's at Rome and the Castle of St. Angelo, seen through the foliage of some light trees on the banks of the Tiber.

M. Alfred Robaut, who is doubtless the greatest authority upon the decorative work of the master, mentions that Corot told him he had at one time painted mural decoration in the Café de Fleurus in Paris ; no traces of these are left, nor does it seem possible to discover any other of his frescoes in Paris, although he appears to have painted several. It seems that from time to time Corot amused himself with the decoration of smaller articles ; he painted some plates and dishes, and some boxes, and even presented to the children of a friend some little brooches, upon which he had painted tiny landscapes. M. Duvelleroy gave him commissions on various occasions to paint a fan, and these were duly executed by him and disposed of.

Of the remainder of his frescoes, two exist in the house of a M. Castagnet at Montlhéry ; three are in the Castle of Gruyères, near Geneva, painted at the request of M. Ballaud ; and one adorns the dining-room of M. Chemouillet at Sèvres. A very beautiful

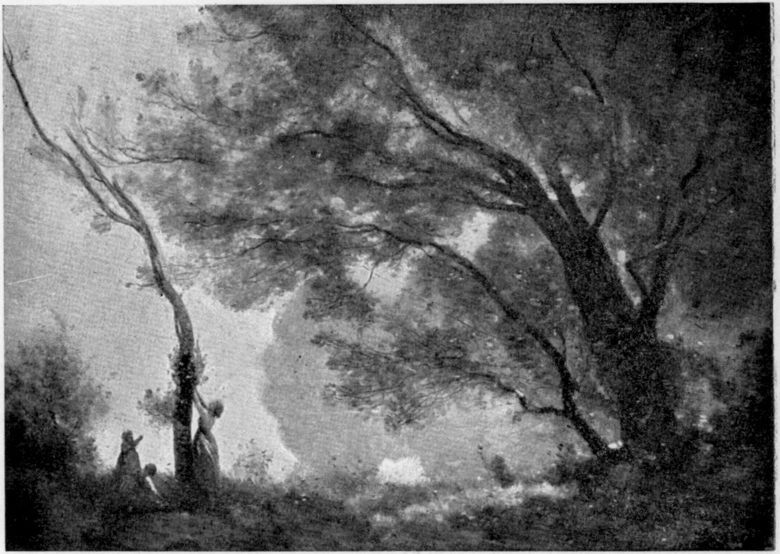

THE LAKE

decorative panel, unearthed for the Posthumous Exhibition, had been designed to be copied in tapestry at the royal manufactory. It was, however, never used for this purpose, and the original now forms one of the chief ornaments of the porcelain factory at Sèvres, where it was finally placed.

Before closing the list of what we may call Corot's miscellaneous works, we cannot refrain from adding an attractive account of the painting of a certain palette which was among the most valued possessions of M. Georges Rodrigues in 1873.

M. Rodrigues, a distinguished amateur artist, greatly admiring Corot's picture of Dante and Virgil, requested the master to make him a replica on a greatly reduced scale. This Corot consented to do, and decided that he would work at M. Rodrigues' house. The small copy being completed, Corot noticed that he had inadvertently left his palette attached like a seal to the corner of the picture. The sight gave him the idea of painting upon the palette some scene to complete, as it were, the transaction. But he was unable to decide upon a suitable subject. He wanted something humorous yet appropriate, which would suggest the original painting left so long to "paper" one corner of his studio wall.

After due consideration he resolved to imagine an entire revulsion of the feeling of indifference with which the "Dante" had been received in 1859, and to depict a crowd pressing so closely around an easel which held his chef-d'œuvre that a whole posse of police had to be called upon to keep order. To enhance the impression Corot then painted himself upon the back of the palette reclining on cushions and smoking a long pipe. "This is a Turk that I have painted," he said doubtfully when the figure was finished; "not very much like me, and very pretentious; I will do it over again"; and on the space occupied by the artist's thumb while painting he drew himself in profile in the act of sketching. At the top of this charming production he wrote a dedication: "To my friend, G. Rodrigues," with the name and date, "Corot, 1873."

ALPHABETICAL LIST OF PICTURES, FRESCOES, AND ETCHINGS,

WITH NAMES OF OWNERS, PUBLIC GALLERIES, AND CHURCHES IN WHICH THEY ARE TO BE FOUND; TOGETHER WITH OTHER NOTES

Adam et Eve chassés du Paradis (fresco). (In the church at Ville d'Avray.)

Apennines, the Route across. (J. S. Forbes, Esq., London.)

Appian Way.

Arcadia, in. (A. P. Forrester Paton, Esq., Scotland.)

Autumn.

Avenue, the. (Messrs. Obach, London.)

Bacchante à la Panthère.

Bain de Diane. (Bordeaux Museum.)

Banks of a stream.

Banks of the Loire.

Banks of the Seine.

Banks of the Seine. (J. S. Forbes, Esq., London.)

Baptism of Christ. (Church of St. Nicholas de Chardonnet, Paris.)

Baptism of Christ by St. John (fresco). (In the church at Ville d'Avray.)

Bateau, le : Effet de lune.

Bateau sous les Saules (etching). (British Museum.)

Bather, the. (James Arthur, Esq., Scotland.)

Bathers, the. (W. A. Coats, Esq., Scotland. Universal Exhibition, 1889, Paris.)

Beffroi de Douai. (Universal Exhibition, 1878, Paris.)

Bent Tree, the. (Alex. Young, Esq., Blackheath.)

Berger jouant avec une chèvre.

Biblis. (Exhibited after Corot's death at the Salon, 1875.)

Birch Trees.

Boatman on the Lake Némi.

Bords du grand Lac à Ville d'Avray. (Rouen Museum.)

Bouquet d'Arbres, le.

Break of Day.

Bridge at Mantes.

Brook, the.

Brook, the, in the Valley.

Bûcherons, les. (Salon, 1875.)

Campagne boissée (etching).

Campagne de Rome, en hiver.

Campagne de Rome.

Canal de St. Quentin. (Isaac Cook, Esq., St. Louis, U.S.A.)

Carp Pond, Fontainebleau. (J. S. Forbes, Esq., London.)

Cascades de Terni, les.

Castel Gondolfo. (Louvre.)

Castle of St. Angelo, Rome. (Universal Exhibition, 1889, Paris.)

Cathédrale de Chartres.

Cavalier, le.

Cavalier tenant une epée.

Cervara, la, Rome.

Chantilly.

Charette, la. (Universal Exhibition of 1889, Paris.)

Château de Baume-la-Rolande.

Château de Fontainebleau.

Château de Thierry.   (H. S. Henry, Esq., Philadelphia.)

Château de Wagnouville.

Chaumières au bord d'un Marais.

Chemin creux avec un cavalier.   (Universal Exhibition, 1889, Paris.)

Chemin montant, le.   (Universal Exhibition, 1889, Paris.)

Cheval, se baignant : Ville d'Avray.

Chevrier, un.   (Lille Museum.)

Chevrèire, la, Italie.

Chevriers, Golfe de Naples.

Child reading.

Christ in the Garden : Mount of Olives (fresco).   (In the church at Ville d'Avray.)

Clair de Lune.

Coliseum, the.   (Louvre.)

Coliseum, the.   (J. S. Forbes, Esq., London.)

Concert, le.

Concert Champêtre.   (Chantilly.)

Cottage, the.

Coubron : The Farmyard.

Coûcher du Soleil.

Coup de Vent, le.

Crayfisher, the.   (James Donald, Esq., Glasgow.)

Crécy en Brie.

Crépuscule.

Dance of Cupids.

Dance of Nymphs.   (Luxemburg.)

Dance of Nymphs.   (New York.)

Dance of Nymphs.

Danse Antique.   (Salon, 1875.)

Dans les Dunes (etching).

Dante et Virgil.   (Louvre.)

Dante et Virgil.   (Boston)

Daphnis et Chloë.

Démocrite et les Abdéritains.

Destruction of Sodom.   (Salon, 1844.)

Diana surprised while bathing.

Diana's bath.   (Universal Exhibition, 1899, Paris.)

Diane à sa toilette.

Dome Florentine (etching).

Don Quichotte et Sancho Panza (decorative panel).
    (Executed for Daubigny.)

Don Quixote: An Episode.   (J. Cowan, Esq., Scotland.)

Drinking-place, the.

Dunes de Zuydcote, les.

Dunkerque.   (J. S. Forbes, Esq., London.)

Edge of the Forest : Morning.

Effet de Neige.   (Universal Exhibition, 1855, Paris.)

Effet du Matin.

Effet du Matin (another).

End of the Valley.   (M. J. Allard, Paris.)

Enfants de la Ferme, les.

Entrée du Village : Zuidcote.   (Messrs. Obach, London.)

Entrée d'un Village.   (M. Detrimônd.)

Environs de Florence.   (Metz Museum.)

Environs de Naples.

Environs de Paris.

Environs de Rouen (etching).

Environs de Ville d'Avray.

Étude à Mery.

Étude à Ville d'Avray.

Étude à Ville d'Avray (another).

Étude à Ville d'Avray (another).

Étude de chênes, Fontainebleau.   (Universal Exhibition,
    1889, Paris.)

Eurydice blessée.   (Universal Exhibition, 1889, Paris.)

Evening.   (Miss Cooper, New York.)

Evening.   (Mme. Cottier, Paris.)

Evening.   (J. J. Cowan, Esq., Edinburgh.)

Evening Glow.   (Alex. Young, Esq., Blackheath.)

Evening in Arcadia.   (J. S. Forbes, Esq., London.)

Evening in Normandy.   (H. Bruce, Esq., Edinburgh.)

Evening : Sunset.   (J. Donald, Esq., Glasgow.)

Evening : Sunset Light.   (J. S. Forbes, Esq., London.)

Evening Star.   (T. S. Walters, Esq., Baltimore.)

Evening Walk, the.   (J. S. Forbes, Esq., London.)

Famille du Moissonneur.

Faneuse.   (Universal Exhibition, 1889, Paris.)

Farm at Toulon.   (A. Spencer, Esq., New York.)

Femme à la perle.   (Universal Exhibition, 1889, Paris.)

Femme assise.   (Universal Exhibition, 1889, Paris.)

Femme dans un atelier.

Femme de la fontaine.

Femme devant un chevalet.

Femme en rouge, jouant de la guitarre.   (Universal
   Exhibition, 1889, Paris.)

Ferry, the.   (James Coats, Esq., Scotland.)

Fête de Village.   (Original lithograph.)

Field of Waterloo.   (J. S. Forbes, Esq., London.)

Fisherman : Autumn.   (J. S. Forbes, Esq., London.)

Fisherman, the.

Fisherman's Wife and Child.

Fishers, the.   (Mme. Acloque, Paris.)

Flight into Egypt.   (Church at Rosny, near Mantes.)

Fontainebleau : The English Garden.   (J. S. Forbes,
   Esq., London.)

Ford, the.   (New York.)

Forêt, une.

Forêt de Coubron, la.
Forêt de Fontainebleau.
Forêt de Fontainebleau (another).
Fortifications de Douai (etching).
French château, A. (J. Anderson, Esq., Glasgow.)

Garibaldi's House, Rome. (J. S. Forbes, Esq., London.)
Gardeuse de Vaches, paysage. (Universal Exhibition,
    1889, Paris.)
Gardeuses de bestiaux au marais.
Gathering flowers : Pastorale.
Gaulois, les, paysage.
Génève, 1852.
Genzano, près de Némi. (Universal Exhibition, 1889,
    Paris.)
Goatherd, the. (Sir Matthew Arthur, Bart., Scotland.)
Goatherds. (Lisbon.)
Goatherd piping. (Louvre.)
Golden Age, the.
Gournay, le gros arbre.
Gros chêne de Fontainebleau.
Gué, le. (Universal Exhibition, 1889, Paris.)
Gust of Wind, A. (A. Young, Esq., Blackheath.)

Hagar in the Desert. (Count Doria.)
Hagar in the Wilderness. (Louvre.)
Hallebardier, le.
Hay-cart, the. (J. S. Forbes, Esq., London.)
Heights of Ville d'Avray.
Homer and the Shepherds. (St. Lo Museum.)

Idylle.
Idylle, rond des enfants. (Archibald Coats, Esq., Paisley.)
Ile d'Ischia, près Naples.

LIST OF PICTURES, ETC. 167

Ile St. Bartolomeo.
Incendie de Sodome.
Intérieur du Bois.
Intérieur d'Eglise.
Intérieur de cuisine, Mantes. (Exposition Universelle de, 1889, Paris.)
Interior of a Cottage at Limousin. (M. Moreau Nélaton, Paris.)
In the Marshes. (P. H. Sears, Esq., Boston.)
Introspection. (J. S. Forbes, Esq., London.)
Italian Girl. (J. S. Forbes, Esq., London.)
Italie : Souvenir.
Italie : Souvenir (etching).
Italie : Vue.
Italy, Souvenir of.

Jeune fille à la mandoline. (Universal Exhibition, 1889, Paris.)
Jeune fille en promenade. (Universal Exhibition, 1889, Paris.)
Jeune fille au bain.
Jeune Grecque.
Jeune mère.
Juive d'Alger, une.

L'Abreuvoir.
Lac du Tyrol (etching).
"La Garde meurt, mais ne ce rend pas." (Original lithograph.)
Lake of Albano.
Lake of Némi. (H. V. Newcomb, Esq., New York.)
Lake of Némi. (M. Hecht, Paris.)
Lake Scene. (Mrs. Elder, Glasgow.)

La Liseuse.

Landscape.

Landscape.   (Lyons Museum.)

Landscape.   (La Rochelle Museum.)

Landscape.   (La Rochelle Museum.)

Landscape.   (Paris.)

Landscape.   (Montpellier Museum.)

Landscape.   (Louvre.)

Landscape.   (Douai Museum.)

Landscape at Evening.

Landscape : Autumn.   (J. S. Forbes, Esq., London.)

Landscape : Morning.   (J. S. Forbes, Esq., London.)

Landscape : Setting Sun.

Landscape : Spring.   (J. S. Forbes, Esq., London.)

Landscape : Study for *Macbeth*.   (J. S. Forbes, Esq., London.)

Landscape with Cattle.   (P. H. Sears, Esq., New York.)

Landscape with Felled Tree.

Landscape with Figures.   (Paris.)

Landscape with Figures (unfinished).   (Boston Museum.)

Landscape with Figures.   (A. Sanderson, Esq., Edinburgh.)

Landscape with Ruined Temple.   (J. S. Forbes, Esq., London.)

La peste de Barcelone.   (Original lithograph)

La petite Vanne.

La Rochelle.   (M. E. May.)

La Rochelle (another).   (M. A. Robaut, Paris.)

La Route.

La Saulaie.

La Source : Étude de fille nue.

L'Atelier.

L'Attente au sentier.

Le bain froid.

Le chariot.

L'Etang.   (John Reid, Esq., Glasgow.)

L'Etang à Ville d'Avray (etching), 1860.

Le lac.   (Louvre.)

Le lac.   (A. Young, Esq., Blackheath.)

Le lac de Garde.

Le lac de Garde (another).

Lever du Soleil.

L'Heure matinale.

Limetz, près Mantes.

Limousin.

Lisière de Bois.

L'Incendie de Paris par les Prussiens, 1870.

Macbeth and the Witches.   (Walters Collection, Baltimore, U.S.A.)

Macbeth and the Witches.   (Wallace Collection, Hertford House, London.)

Madeleine en prière (fresco).   (In the church at Ville d'Avray.)

Mademoiselle Rosalie.   (Original lithograph.)

Mantes.

Marais, le.

Marais près de la Ferme, le.   (J. Inglis, Esq., Glasgow.)

Marchand de Cochon.   (Messrs. Obach, London.)

Marcoussy.   (Purchased by Napoleon III.)

Marcoussy, près Montlhèry.   (Universal Exhibition, 1855.)

Marine, une.   (Royal Museum, Brussels.)

Marisselle, près Beauvais.   (Alf. Marme, Tours.)

Martignes.

Matin, le.

Matin, au bord du lac.   (J. S. Forbes, Esq., London.)

Matinée.

Matinée en Italie.

Matinée, une.

Matinée, une (pastorale). (Louvre.)

Matinée, une : Ville d'Avray.

Matin sur l'étang : Ville d'Avray.

Méditation.

Moine, un.

Moonrise. (W. A. Coats, Esq., Scotland.)

Morning. (Ionides Collection, South Kensington.)

Mortefontaine.

Mother and Child.

Moulin de Saint Nicholas.

Moulin Drocourt.

Naples. (Exposition Universelle, 1889.)

Narni.

Némi : Peinture murale chez M. Robert.

Normandie, effet de Soir. (H. Bruce, Esq.)

Nymphe couchée au bord de la mer.

Nymphe couchée au bord de la mer (another).

Nymphe des bois.

Nymphes au bain.

Nymphes jouant avec un tigre.

Nymphes et Faunes. (Exposition Universelle, 1889.)

Nymphs dancing. (Vanderbilt, Esq., New York.)

Nymphs of the Dawn. (Mrs. Fell, Philadelphia.)

Nymphs playing with Cupid.

Old Cottage at Semur.

Old Farmhouse. (J. Staats Forbes, Esq., London.)

On the Banks of the Seine. (J. Staats Forbes, Esq.,
London.)

On the Seine. (J. Staats Forbes, Esq., London.)

Orchard, the (Ville de Semur).

Orphée.

Orphée entraînant Eurydicée.
Outskirts of the Wood.
Outskirts of the Ville d'Avray.

Palazzo Doria, Genoa. (Exposition Universelle, 1889.)
Parc des Lions a Pont-Marly. (Exposition Universelle, 1889.)
Passage du Gué. (Exposition Universelle, 1889.)
Passeur, le.
Pastorale. (Exposition Universelle, 1889.)
Pastorale. (J. S. Forbes, Esq., London.)
Pastorale, Souvenir d'Italie. (Glasgow Art Gallery.)
Pasture and Pond.
Pâturage. (Messrs. Obach, London.)
Paysage. (Louvre.)
Paysage composé (drawing). (Musée de Lille.)
Paysage d'Artois. (Exposition Universelle, 1889.)
Peasant riding. (M. E. Lyons, Brussels.)
Peasants at a Pool.
Pêcheur à la ligne.
Pêcheur Napolitain.
Perpignan. (J. S. Forbes, Esq., London.)
Petits dénicheurs, les. (Exposition Universelle, 1878.)
Picardie, la.
Plaine humide en Flândres.
Plaisirs du Soir, les.
Pond at Ville d'Avray.
Pond at Ville d'Avray, with Corot's House. (J. S. Forbes, Esq.)
Pont, le.
Port of Marseilles. (J. S. Forbes, Esq.)
Portraits of Corot's Father and Mother. (J. S. Forbes, Esq.)
Poule aux œufs d'or.

Prairie à Ste. Catherine-les-Arraz.

Près Arras.

Printemps. (Exposition Universelle, 1855.) (G. Coats, Esq., Ayr.)

Rageur dans la plaine, Fontainebleau.

Ramasseurs de bois.

Ramasseuse de fagôts, Ville d'Avray.

Ravine, A.

Reed-cutter, the.

Reed-cutting. (J. S. Forbes, Esq., London.)

Reed-cutting (unfinished sketch). (J. S. Forbes, Esq., London.)

Repos, le.

Repos, le. (J. S. Forbes, Esq.)

Rest.

Retour du marché d'Arras.

Riva, vue de.

Rive verte. (Exposition Universelle, 1878.)

Rivière de Scarpe.

Rivière près Beauvais.

Road to the Church.

Rome. (Baron Denys Cochin, Paris.)

Rome, near to (etching).

Rome : The Campagna at Night.

Rome : Fontaine en face de l'Académie. (" Vente Corot.")

Ronde de danseuses au bord de l'eau.

Ronde de Nymphes. (M. Barbedienne.)

Rouen Cathedral. (J. S. Forbes, Esq., London.)

Route d'Arras. (Louvre.)

Route ensoleillée.

Route, la, paysage.

Route de Sêvres. (Louvre.)

Rue de Village en Picardie.

Ruin, the. (Hamilton Bruce, Esq., Edinburgh.)

Ruines du Château de Pierrefonds. (Exposition Universelle, 1867.)

St. Jérôme. (Church at Ville d'Avray.)

St. Peters from the Pincio. (J. S. Forbes, Esq., London.)

St. Sebastian: Martyrdom. (T. S. Walters, Esq., Baltimore.)

St. Sebastien et les Saintes Femmes. (Exposition Universelle, 1878.)

Saintry.

Sandpit, the. (M. J. Ferry.)

Scene from *Les Hugenots*. (J. S. Forbes, Esq., London.)

Seine à Châlon.

Shepherd's Star. (Toulouse Museum.)

Silène.

Site d'Italie.

Site d'Italie.

Site du Limousin.

Sluice, the (etching).

Soir.

Soir, le.

Soir, le.

Soir, un.

Soirée, une. (Exposition Universelle, 1855.)

Soleil Couchant. (J. S. Lankenan, Philadelphia.)

Soleil Couchant, Tyrol Italien.

Soleil Couchant.

Soleil Couchant, Ville d'Avray.

Soleil Levant.

Soleil Levant.

Solitude: Limousin. (Mme. de Cassin.)

Solitude (etching).

Souvenir d'Arleux du Nord. (M. Robaut.)

Souvenir de Coubron.

Souvenir d'Italie (etching). (Messrs. Obach, London.)

Souvenir d'Italie.

Souvenir de Normandie.

Souvenir de Toscane (etching). (Messrs. Obach, London.)

Souvenir de Ville d'Avray.

Souvenir de Ville d'Avray.

Souvenir du lac de Némi.

Storm on the Sandhills.

Stream : Woman and Child (decorative panel). (Painted
    for Daubigny.)

Study for the Picture of la Bacchante.

Sunset.

Tempé à Ville d'Avray, une.

Tivoli : From the Villa d'Este. (M. Henri Rouart,
    Paris.)

Toilette, la. (M. V. Desfossés.)

Tombs of the Cæsars. (J. S. Forbes, Esq., London.)

Torrent dans les Romagnes.

Toscane.

Tour de Montlhèry. (Messrs. Obach, London.)

Tournant de la Seine à Pont-Marly.

Towing-path. (J. S. Forbes, Esq.)

Trees and Pond. (A. T. Reid, Esq., Glasgow.)

Tréport : Au plage. (Exposition Universelle, 1889.)

Trois Vâches à l'Etang.

Twilight. (Ionides Collection, South Kensington.)

Tyrol Italien. (J. S. Forbes, Esq.)

Tyrol Italien.

Vâches à l'Abreuvoir.

Venus et Cupid

Venus coupe les Ailes de l'Amour (etching).

Verger, le.

Vieux Pont de Poissy. (Messrs. Obach, London.)

View at Biarritz. (M. Seymour, Paris.)

View of the Coliseum, Rome. (Erwin Davis, Esq., New York.)

View of the Forum, Rome. (Louvre.)

View of the Tyrol. (Marseilles Museum.)

View of Ville d'Avray. (Rouen Museum.)

Village Street.

Village of Marcoussy. (Exposition Universelle, 1855.)

Villa Pamphili, Rome. (W. Quilter, Esq., London.)

Ville d'Avray. (J. S. Forbes, Esq.)

Ville d'Avray. (M. J. C. Roux, Marseilles.)

Ville d'Avray. (Mrs. Hemenway, Boston.)

Ville et lac de Coîne. (Exposition Universelle, 1889.)

Vue d'Artois. (Exposition Universelle, 1889.)

Vue de Corbeil : De grand matin.

Vue de Furia, Ile d'Ischia.

Vue d'Italie. (Avignon Museum.)

Vue d'Italie (etching).

Vue de la Forêt de Fontainebleau. (Exposition Universelle, 1889.)

Vue de Rotterdam.

Vue de Suisse.

Vue du Village de Sin, près Douai.

Vue de Volterra, Toscane.

Vue prise à Ville d'Avray.

Vue prise à Volterra, Toscane.

Waterloo : The Field of. (J. S. Forbes, Esq., London.)

Wild Man of the Woods. (J. Cowan, Esq., Glasgow.)

Willows.

Woman and Tiger.

Women bathing.
Wood-gatherers.   (Corcoran Gallery, Washington.)
Wood and Lake.   (Potter Palmer, Esq., Chicago.)
Woods of Marcoussy.   (Erwin Davis, Esq., New York.)

Zuidcote.   (Messrs. Obach, London.)

NOTE.—It must be remembered that many of these pictures
are constantly changing hands even as we write.

PICTURES EXHIBITED IN SALONS

ARRANGED ACCORDING TO DATE

1827

Campagne de Rome
Narni

1831

Cervara, la, Rome
Forêt de Fontainebleau
Vue de Furia, Ile d'Ischia
Convent on the Adriatic

1833

Madeleine en prière

1834

Une Forêt
Une Marine
Site d'Italie

1835

Hagar in the Wilderness
Vue de Riva

1836

Campagne de Rome en
  hiver
Diana surprised while
  Bathing

1837

Ile d'Ischia, près Naples
Soleil couchant

1838

Silène
Vue de Volterra, Toscane

1839

Landscape at Evening
St. Jérôme
Souvenir d'Italie

1840

Flight into Egypt
Landscape : Setting Sun
Un Moine

1841

Démocrite et les abdéri-
  tains
Environs de Naples
Une Matinée : Pastorale

1842

Effet du Matin
Site d'Italie

1843

Jeunes filles au bain
Un Soir

1844

Destruction of Sodom

Landscape with Figures

Rome : The Campagna at
Night

1845

Daphnis and Chloë

Homer and the Shepherds

Paysage

Le Verger

1846

Forêt de Fontainebleau

1847

Berger jouant avec une
chèvre

Landscape

1848

Crépuscule

Intérieur de Bois

Vue d'Italie

Sunset

Soir

Effet du Matin

1849

Christ in the Garden of
Olives

Coliseum

Site de Limousin

Vue prise à Ville d'Avray

Vue prise à Volterra

1850

Étude à Ville d'Avray

Lever du Soleil

Une Matinée

Soleil couchant : Tyrol
italien

1852

La Rochelle

Soleil couchant

1853

Matinée

Martyrdom of Saint Se-
bastian

Coucher du Soleil

1857

Le Concert

Incendie de Sodome

Une Matinée : Ville d'Avray

Nymphs Playing with
Cupid

Souvenir de Ville d'Avray

1859

Dante and Virgil

Étude à Ville d'Avray

Idylle

Limousin

Macbeth

Tyrol italien

1861

Souvenir d'Italie

Le Lac

Nymphs Dancing

Orphée

Le repos

Soleil levant

1863
Étude à Ville d'Avray
Étude à Méry
Soleil levant

1864
Le coup de vent
Mortefontaine
Shepherd's Star

1865
Souvenir d'Italie (etching)
Le Matin
Souvenir du lac de Nemi

1866
Environs de Rome (etching)
Solitude : Limousin

1867
A Gust of Wind
Marisselle, près Beauvais

1868
Matin : Ville d'Avray
Le Soir

1869
La Liseuse
Souvenir de Ville d'Avray

1872
Près Arras
Soleil couchant : Ville d'Avray

1873
Le Passeur

1874
Clair de Lune
Souvenir d'Arleux du Nord

1875
Biblis
Les Bûcherons
Les Plaisirs du Soir

BIBLIOGRAPHY

Academy. 1874. P. Burty.

Academy. 1875. October. Frederick Wedmore.

Album Classique des Chefs-d'Œuvre de Corot (Essai critique). L. Roger-Milès.

Art and Letters. Vol. i. 1881. Vol. ii. 1882.

L'Art Contemporain. 1868. Chaumelin.

L'Art. 1875. J. Rousseau.

L'Art. 1875. E. Daliphard.

L'Art. 1879. A. Robaut.

L'Art. 1882. A. Robaut.

L'Art et les Artistes Modernes. 1864. Chesneau.

Les Artistes de mon temps. 1876. Ch. Blanc.

Art Journal. 1867. July.

Art Journal. 1875.

Art Journal. 1889. July. R. A. M. Stevenson.

Art Journal. Vol. xiii. Poem by A. L. Salmon.

Athenæum. 1875. February.

L'Autographe au Salon. 1864.

The Barbizon School of Painters. Vol. i. 1889. ("Great Artists.") J. W. Mollett.

Les Beaux-Arts à l'Exposition. 1878. Ch. Blanc.

"Camille Corot." 1891. (*Les Artistes Célèbres.*) L. Roger-Milès.

La capitale de l'Art. 1886. Albert Wolff.

Causeries du Louvre. 1834. "Jal."

Cent Chefs-d'Œuvre des Collections Parisiennes. 1884. A. Wolff.

Century Magazine. 1889. June. M. G. van Rensselaer.

Contemporary Review. Vol. xxvi. 1875. June. J. Comyns Carr.

"Corot." (*Peintres et Sculpteurs Contemporains.*) 1884. Jules Clarétie.

"Corot." *Souvenirs intimes.* 1875. H. Dumesnil.

"Corot and Millet." (Special Winter Number of the *Studio.* 1902-3.)

"Corot." (*Les Artistes Modernes.*) Eugène Montrosier.

"Corot." (*Galerie Contemporaine.*) A. Robaut.

"Corot." Suivi d'un appendice par A. Robaut. 1884. (*Bibliothèque d'Art Moderne.*) Jean Rousseau.

"Corot." *The Barbizon School of Painters.* 1892. David Croal Thomson.

Douze Croquis et dessins : par Corot. 1872.

Douze Lithographies d'après Corot. 1870. (Notice par P. Burty.) E. Vernier.

L'Eau-forte en 1875. Philippe Burty.

L'Eau-forte en 1875. E. Montrosier.

Eclectic Magazine. Vol. cxxvi. 1896. May.

Exposition de l'Œuvre de Corot. 1875. (Notice Biographique.) P. Burty.

Le Figaro. February 24th. 1875. A. Marx.

Galerie Durand Ruel. (28 gravures.) Armand Silvestre.

Gazette des Beaux Arts. 1859. P. Mantz.

Gazette des Beaux Arts. 1861. P. Mantz.

Gazette des Beaux Arts. 1873. R. Ménard.

Gazette des Beaux Arts. 1875. J. Buisson.

Histoire des Artistes Vivants. 1862. Théophile Silvestre.

Histoire des Peintres Français. Ch. Blanc.

Histoire des Peintres. 1861. W. Bürger.

Magazine of Art. 1888. D. C. Thomson.

Maitres et Petits-Maitres. 1877. P. Burty.

Millet et Corot. 1876. Ph. L. Couturier.

Modern Painting. 1893. George Moore.

New England Magazine. Vol. v. (N. S.) C. Thurweinger.

New Review. Vol. xiv. R. A. M. Stevenson.

Notes et Souvenirs. 1889. Ludovic Halévy.

Old and New. Vol. x. A. H. Bicknell.

Overland Monthly. Vol. xv. J. P. Moore.

Peintres Contemporains. 1888. Charles Bigot.

Peintres Romantiques. A. Chesneau.

Peintres et Sculpteurs Contemporains. Jouast.

Portfolio. 1870. p. 60.

Portfolio. 1875. René-Ménard. p. 146.

Revue des Musées. 1889. October.

Salons de T. Thoré. Avec une preface par W. Bürger. 1868.

Six Portraits. 1889. M. G. van Rensselaer.

Souvenirs Intimes. "Corot." 1875. Henri Dumesnil.

Studio. Vol. i. 1893. "Study of Recent Art." R. A. M. Stevenson.

Voyage à travers l'Exposition des Beaux Arts. 1855. Edmond About.

INDEX

PLYMOUTH
WILLIAM BRENDON AND SON
PRINTERS